SINCE VICTOR HUGO

This book is a translation
from the French work of Bernard Faÿ entitled
PANORAMA DE LA LITTERATURE
CONTEMPORAINE

Since
Victor Hugo

FRENCH LITERATURE OF TO-DAY

By

BERNARD FAŸ

Translated by
PAUL RICE DOOLIN

KENNIKAT PRESS, INC./PORT WASHINGTON, N. Y.

Contents

v

SINCE VICTOR HUGO

CHAPTER I

Introductory

MINGLED with the natural admiration which we have for ourselves, are strange modesties. We would scarce allow a foreigner to say that our railroads or our cheeses are inferior to those of his country; but many of us would admit as a matter of course that "our modern literature is unintelligible", or that in the last fifty years nothing has been done comparable to the things of yesterday. Many Frenchmen consider that we have had no "great writers" since Taine and Renan; they are ignorant of what has happened since 1880. This is a constant source of surprise to cultivated minds in foreign countries, who look upon France's literature as one of her principal titles to glory. In Germany, England, America, Japan, our Symbolists were read, our Naturalists sold by the million. Claudel was played in Germany before he was known in Paris. Cubism aroused

3

wondrous admiration, and Dada brought forth vibrant commentaries, formal investigation, imitations. For fifty years our literature has been the great curiosity of the world. During this period it has done more for the renewal of ideas, sentiments, artistic techniques throughout the universe than at any other moment in our history. Failure to take advantage of this is either modesty or excessive stupidity.

We are not at home in our own house. It is easier to understand Paris from New York or Tokio than from Versailles. Since 1880 the Schools have come too fast, and the great men invented too much. Our logical genius has not had time to draw up an exact and satisfactory catalogue. The public is suffering from a sort of headache, the universities are silent, and the newspapers confuse everything with "piquant" and contradictory details. The France of 1927 is a strange kaleidoscope. If one were to make a literary chart, like the charts of dialects, races, agricultural products, it would show all the colors in the rainbow.

In Paris, at certain points, bright red spots would indicate the places where the literature of to-day lives so intensely that it never settles; then the more peaceful quarters where something of Symbolism still lingers, those where Naturalism has maintained itself, those which are still tinged with Romanticism. Then, at the gates of Paris, a sharp change, and vast spaces where reign the literatures of 1880, of 1830, 1750, 1660, 1550, and before. Some districts, because of their misty skies and natural spirituality, have remained faithful to Symbolism, like Wallonie; Romanticism is citadeled in certain provincial towns, especially in the South whence, suddenly, it invades us, and the Middle Ages, more discreet, eye us from their refuge in the archeological societies of the chief towns of the cantons. All these ages coëxist, and the thing which for the centuries to come will be "to-day" lives only in a few houses of an enormous city, incapable of throwing its light very far, able only to illuminate a few other houses in London, New York and Peking, until at last it reach Gap and Quimperlé. Out of this come cruel confusion and misunderstanding between people of the same stock, who employ the same words, but not the same ideas nor the same sentiments, and who will continue to impeach one another until the day when, all being dead, posterity the order-maker assumes all to have been alike and invests them all with the capes of M. Proust and the forelock of M. Barrès.

The penetration of literature varies with the place and the social group. There might be a literary geography and a literary geology. When groups of the Parisian "aristocracy" had already learned to be Cubists, the bourgeoisie continued to delight in Symbolism, and, in the subway, the shopgirls were still reading Naturalist novels, while the apprentices preferred the adventures of Sherlock Holmes. Whatever your politics, it must be admitted, whether you will or no, that the "higher classes" adapt themselves much more quickly to new literary theories, even when those theories carry their condemnation and aim at their destruction. The navy, diplomacy, and the bar are much more supple intellectually than the army or the magistracy or politics. This rule applies to all nations of the world and is particularly true for France.

Introductory

After all, literature is a luxury, and only those can afford a very new literature who are very rich, very free, and entirely disengaged from material care. Romanticism was hatched by the salons, as had been the doctrine of 1660, and that of "Fine Language" thirty years before. Symbolism was an aristocratic doctrine. The Russian ballets, Cubism, Marcel Proust were vogues before they were recognized by the crowd, the newspapers and the critics. From time to time a poor young man presumes to the pleasure of doing better than the rich and being newer than they, but usually he pays for his venture a great price, his life. And there you are.

Still one might dissipate the misunderstanding which hides from us the wealth of our immediate past. It would be well if some one, still free, and constantly penetrated by the grandeur of what he ought to praise, might show in a brief sketch the procession of ideas, manners and men across our literature since 1880, since the moment when, gradually, the ditch was dug between prose and verse, between the poetry of those who know and the prose of those who sell, the work of the genius and the product of the tradesman — Arthur Rimbaud and Georges Ohnet — since the moment when first there was a distinction made between a literature for the crowd and another for the élite.

In fact it would seem that since 1880 prose and verse have been engaged in a strange war for the conquest of the attention of the public. The poets, by a constantly exaggerated striving for novelty, have aimed to astonish, surprise, fascinate. The prose writers in all fields, faithful to a tradition old in France, have proposed to follow step by step all the movements in public opinion and manners, to have a language the most faithful to the group, the most objective and social ever seen on this earth, and the Academy, originally founded to this end, has encouraged them in this inclination. This body, which often has not shared the political opinions of the régime or of the Government, has shown itself much more prudent in literature, and in the domain which might be considered its own, has given proof of surprising reserve.

Introductory

None of the writers which the generations between fifteen and thirty years of age recognize as their masters belong to the Academy: Péguy and Proust died without entering; neither Romain Rolland nor Gide is to be seen there, nor Claudel nor Maurras (all of quite different "colors"), while lofty chairs are occupied by historians without influence on the public mind, without "radiation", by soldiers and lawyers, respected, but with little voice in literary affairs. It has not been sufficiently noticed that this evil, the first symptoms of which go back to the end of the eighteenth century, has become acute only in our time. Balzac, Stendhal, Flaubert and Baudelaire were not members of the Academy, but it opened its doors to the leaders of Romanticism, then the young and living literature. In our days the divorce is complete between the Academy and modern literature. This abstention of the Academy consecrates the misunderstanding, it establishes officially the conflict between the genres in prose and poetry, the literature for the use of the social group and the literature for the individual, the author laureate and the author creator. An opposition so irreducible, the traces of which are constantly to be met in French life, cannot be ignored.

For this reason, in the study to which we are about to devote ourselves, we will separate the prose writers and the poets. In presenting the filiation of ideas we will be careful always to offer men as types, and each one of our essays will contain the portrait of a writer, a true image added to the text, for in the person alone does the idea attain its full projection, and it would be too arbitrary not to consider them together. We will follow step by step the three periods which have succeeded one another since 1880: the Symbolist and Naturalist period (1880 to 1900), the Eclectic period (1900 to 1914), the period of the War and the After-War, with the terrible ills which battle and suffering have sown among us, and the inventions which have forced themselves upon us.

For each period we will give a rapid and exact study of the prose, of the poetry, and of the authors in whom the new techniques and ideas are most clearly engraved. We will join to each one of the eighteen studies of the series a bibliography, indicating the books which are most characteristic, and most useful for the understanding of these years.

These notes aim to be neither learned nor singular, but useful, simple and true. In the task we undertake it is of prime importance to present the clear image. To explain a literature is, above all, to furnish means of seeing and discerning, to create associations of ideas and new sensations. One never explains a work as the author has conceived it, for that explanation is the work itself and the work alone, but one can attach it to series of ideas and sentiments which are more general, more social, and through which the group has a hold upon it. Hence we must constantly simplify, enlarge, abridge and systematize. We will strive, nevertheless, to maintain the exact proportions between the various objects, so that the reliefs stand out sharp, but still not deformed in relation to the whole. As far as possible we will follow the chronological order, for the main fault of the books already written on the same or analogous subjects is that they have not remained faithful to that order, with the result that the events are confused, and only a reader already acquainted with French literature can follow the explanations and theories they contain. We would ask nothing of the reader but a few moments of his attention and curiosity, but on our side, we are quite ready to assume that the reader does not know what we are about to say, and embarks in the book as on a voyage of discovery.

It is easy and natural for me to present our literature as a new land which man enters for the first time, for after many travels and absences, coming back from distant countries and plunging again into Paris, I have suddenly reëntered an intellectual world which I had come to consider no longer my own, and in which I now move as a stranger, among goods which do not belong to me and friends from whom I am henceforth to be separated by the space of a lifetime. It is pleasant to feel myself a wayfarer among things whose value and secret contexture I understand, but for which I do not judge myself responsible. It is a source of pride and repose for me to come back home and be there no more than a guest, held to a politeness which takes away nothing from liberty, subject rather to the laws of courtesy than to those of society.

It is in this spirit that I hope to lead you among the books and the men, belonging to no group, to no School, to no review, free of all past, and seeking only to see clear.

CHAPTER II

The Legacy of Victor Hugo

In 1872 France had just changed governments. She was in process of transforming her prose, which was becoming "Naturalist", and was groping toward the discovery of a new poetry.

Before starting on our journey through modern French literature, let us observe certain traits of our character which will help us see clear in the events. The Frenchman, born sly, with a precise and logical mind, has always established clear, sharp distinctions between the various kinds of literature. He looks on prose as an instrument for the understanding of himself and making himself understood to others; hence he has constantly striven to render it more exact, more analytical, more logical, and also he wants it always well adapted to contemporary social and political modes, so that it serve them and express them effectively. Our great classical prose was formed at the same time that the kingdom was centralized; Romantic prose was born amid the upheavals of the Revolution. We will return to the transformations of our prose; it is enough here to note that it is eminently social, utilitarian, and intellectual.

Poetry in France satisfies an entirely different instinct. We worship poetry, in spite of the fact that the foreigner considers us the "driest" people in the world. But our poetry is not like that of other nations, made of frenzy, effusion, pantheism, born of the need of getting out of oneself. Invincibly it turns inward. Despite all his efforts, the Frenchman has never been able to interest himself in externals, in objects; only man, his intimate life and his passions, can make him thrill with joy, fear, æsthetic pleasure. Thus across the ages our poetry constantly returns to love, psychology, the contemplation of the soul, to spiritual, intellectual and logical emotion. We love Ronsard because of his tenderness, Racine for his passions, Marivaux for his sentiments, Voltaire and Beaumarchais for their ideas.

France accepted Romanticism because it gave the individual a new means of enjoying himself, of defending himself against the outside. Every stage in French poetry is marked by the introduction of an original manner of comprehending, defining, and describing the inner life.

Romanticism offered priceless discoveries. After two centuries of analysis and logic, it brought France a religious poetry. Up to 1789, it was the priest who prayed, preached, and alone had the right to touch certain profound emotions. It took a Protestant and a foreigner like Rousseau to dare usurp his prerogatives. The Revolution decapitated the priests, Napoleon made functionaries out of them, and the Viscount de Chateaubriand had the idea of putting the poets in their place. These last would henceforth choose the things to be adored. The poetic domain would be limited no longer to the human passions as defined in the catechism. It would include everything. The poet became a Magian. In France, as everywhere, Romanticism opened with a religious and spiritual crusade: Hugo, Vigny, Lamartine and Lamennais (1820 to 1830).

But Hugo's health, his early and lucky marriage (he married without money at twenty, and by forty-three had won the titles of Academician, Viscount, Peer of France, and the fortune of a millionaire), his success, his extraordinary eloquence, his lack of inner culture and spiritual desire, led him to define French Romanticism as a verbal reformation. He was the most fecund, the most adroit, the most married and the healthiest of our Romantics; he became the leader of the School and, between 1830 and 1840, thanks to his efforts, the country accepted Romantic poetry as a rhetorical discipline. Vigny, voluntary exile, and Lamennais, embroiled with the Church, made no protest. There was nothing left but a grandiloquent, sonorous and social Hugo.

Hugo was not stupid. It took him less than twenty-four years and three revolutions to see his error. Aided by exile and misfortune he did his best to correct it. Since he was a specialist in the word, he deified the word. From 1852 to his death Hugo preached the unity of the world, whose vibrant center is the poet, God all-powerful and creator, master of those legions of angels, words, which he gives men for their succor, inspiration and government. Besides, the poet is himself only a collection of words. Everything is word: ideas, society, God Himself:

Car le mot c'est le Verbe et le Verbe c'est Dieu.

Hence there is everywhere unity, equality, divinity.

The school which succeeded Romanticism, the Parnasse, accepted these principles. It was a staid and sorry school, not that it lacked talent: people like Leconte de Lisle, Hérédia, Banville himself, were good writers and great ones, but they took over from the last Romantics their conception of a unitary world, uniform and dull. Their sole preoccupation was to speak. To be sure, some of them, solicited by the present, by ambition or conscience, tried to describe their souls, like Sully Prudhomme, who was a "fine gentleman" but a "little and monotonous poet", or to sing the crowds, like Coppée, whose "Grève des Forgerons" had such a resounding success around 1871. In these verses could be seen an effort toward a popular poetry at a moment when the masses were raising their head, but in all this there was a misconception. Coppée spoke of the people with a certain vulgarity, but he did not make the people speak, their profound and brutal power.

The error of the Parnassians was serious; they tried to make over expression, when it was the inspiration itself which should have been renewed. This error was the more inexcusable since one of their contemporaries might have shown them their futility, had they listened.

Charles Baudelaire could have supplemented Hugo. He was endowed with infinite sensibility. Without contributing many changes to the form of our poetry (rhyme, cesura, figures, etc.) he revolutionized the content by creating a consciousness more complex, more spacious. The "Fleurs du Mal" (1857) gave the élite the desired elements. Instead of shading off and weakening all differences, keeping only those of value for rhetorical purposes, as did Hugo, Baudelaire perceived them all, expressed them, exaggerated them, lived for them. He was the scene of a constant struggle between vice and virtue, the conscious and the subconscious, the ego and the universe. He rejected nothing and confused nothing. And so his poetry swarms with fabulous agreements, with evocations, with contrasts, and his psychology is the most powerful to be found in any French poet since Racine. I cannot resist citing three lines which show his extraordinary powers of perception and evocation:

Il est des parfums frais comme des chairs d'enfants,
Doux comme les hautbois, verts comme les prairies
— Et d'autres, corrompus, riches et triomphants . . .

Since Baudelaire was a musician, an impeccable stylist, his work, rich in matter as perfect in form, dazzled the youth of 1865- 1880. He lacked, doubtless, only the consciousness of his originality, the will to affirm it as law, instead of displaying it as a phenomenon, to possess all the attributes of genius and become the leader of a School.

But this he was not. The only leader in these last years of the nineteenth century was Hugo. He was looked upon as an institution.

He was sovereign master of French literature. Living retired in splendid isolation with his faithful mistress Juliette Drouet, in his residence Avenue d'Eylau (now Avenue Victor Hugo), he was a sublime bourgeois figure. As perfect a husband as he was an accomplished lover, as great a democrat as poet inspired by the gods. He had no rival. He was the Great Man, the Sibyl of Cumae and the Eiffel Tower all in one.

The young men of 1870–1880 read Baudelaire greedily and hoped to draw from him the poetry which they needed. But each new book of Hugo's burst like a clap of thunder ("Légende des Siècles", 1877 and 1883, "Quatre Vents de l'Esprit", 1881). He surprised, terrified, fascinated everybody. They read him eagerly, and they would have given anything to escape the domination of the hero whom they admired so much, and of whom they were so tired.

BOOKS

V. Hugo: "Les Contemplations."
Baudelaire: "Les Fleurs du Mal."
Hérédia: "Les Trophées."

CHAPTER III

ARTHUR RIMBAUD

Initiator of a New Poetry

WE find traces of Arthur Rimbaud at the threshold of our contemporary literature. He would not stay. He departed in disgust, fury, but if the door swings wide before us, it is because he opened it.

I love him and respect him. It costs me great effort to summon up his image: one would like to leave in peace those one loves, or at least not drag them into our adventures after their death, especially when they have struggled so desperately to preserve "free their adversity." But we cannot rob him of his glory nor alleviate his suffering. He stepped forward when all others failed. He is responsible for what has happened since. In him I see a very great man even more than a man of letters, and thus I shall paint him.

Arthur Rimbaud

One might speak of him in another tone, but Rimbaud is for me an "apostle" and the rest matters little.

Imagine a child, not in the least beautiful, but hard and marvelous, because of his body, glance, his manner of moving, and a strength of unknown resources. He is born in the Ardennes, at Charleville, October 20, 1854. His father, an infantry captain, pays little attention to his children. His mother, intelligent, strong, brutal, desires happiness for him, wealth, power. She is proud of him, and pushes him. He is a clean child, well-behaved, pious, but hardly gentle. His rages are infrequent but violent. He has the ability to win all the prizes, and the will. At the lycée in Charleville his teachers are proud of him (1865–1870).

One day suddenly awakens in him a new life, sex. It seems to inflame his senses, intelligence, imagination (1869). It is then that Rimbaud writes the poems now grouped at the beginning of his "Works" (*Mercure de France*). He has fallen under Romantic and Naturalist influences. His style is violent, glittering, realistic. Already he has genius, but not yet his own. Whatever the beauty of these verses, he later disavowed them too completely for me to consider that I have the right to pause before them. By this time he had met a young professor who exercised the greatest influence over him, Georges Izambart, and who showed him phases of existence he did not know: Democracy, Romanticism, Socialism; it was for him and through him that Rimbaud composed his first works.

The year 1870 brings a new upheaval in the life of the adolescent. Rimbaud visits Paris furtively (August–September, 1870); he decides to escape from his mother and Charleville. Two failures do not discourage him: his mind is made up. His ambition, now conscious of itself and taut, defines its ends. He does not hesitate. He aims straight at the enemy. He attacks God. He would surpass the whole world and even Him. He feels his strength. He will create a new humanity. "To the poet is entrusted humanity and even the animals; he must see to it that his inventions are felt, touched, listened to." (Letter to G. Izambart, May 15, 1871.) Man must be changed, and God. That is the only task worthy the poet, the cause to which the great Romantics were sworn, and which they betrayed. Rimbaud will take their place, succeed where they failed.

The writers of the eighteenth century have taught him that man can be transformed by education. From Nerval, Baudelaire, and his own instinct, he has learned that beyond the realm of ideas and sentiments there is an obscure and truly dominating force, which rules our will and our tastes. Some call it the "soul." It is through this force that God takes possession of man.

Here will Rimbaud join battle; he will change the world, he will remove good and evil, the notion of sin and remorse; he will introduce new sentiments and unknown delights. "The poet will define that quantity of the unknown which during his time arises in the universal soul." He will invent new senses for men, he will give them new bodies, and new souls. He will make them "children of the sun" and himself will be the "stealer of fire."

Naïvely, at first he had desired to destroy the social edifice with the Communards, but he was soon forced to despise these petty revolutionists, pinched, lacking in real ambition. A trip to Paris, during which he enlisted with the Commune, (March, 1871), educated Rimbaud by disillusion. Henceforth he will go farther. He burns his bridges. He quits family, teachers, women, even his friends (December, 1871). Free at last he goes to live in Paris, where, so he thinks, everything is possible. There he meets a poet named Verlaine, a sort of animal in whom that obscure domain where Rimbaud would be king has a richness, amplitude, vitality which he has never known. Verlaine becomes for Rimbaud the necessary instrument, the clay to mold, the true wife from whom he will get his posterity. With one move Rimbaud has captured Verlaine: intelligence, soul, desire. They live together, in contempt of everything and everybody, thirsting only to create their world. They travel (journey in Belgium and to London, July to November, 1872); they compose poems such as none had made before. These poems are not born of the contact with things, as had been everything imagined before, but spring from the *place where there are no things, but only desires*, and they aim to create beings, not to imitate them. "Poetry will no longer rhythm action", Rimbaud had announced to Izambart in May, 1871, "it will march on ahead." He keeps his promise. To persuade he does not reason, he sings; to delight he does not flatter old habits, he proffers inventions. Rimbaud cultivates, orders and disorders all his senses, so that he may know and feel all that has been known and felt before, obtain the perfect delectation which comes from the total possession of self, and from the faculty of producing in oneself and others the state of being one has chosen. It is then that he composes the poems in verse and prose collected subsequently under the name "Illuminations", and which are the only works he recognized in the fullness of his genius.

To win in this struggle he spares nothing, neither work nor disgust, violence nor blasphemy. By the end of a year it becomes exhausting. His strength is worn away. Suddenly he notices that men turn away from him. His friend Verlaine is afraid, and he himself weakens. Then he tries to free himself from the world which has taken so much from him. He wants to go away; to this end he engages in mysterious businesses, but Verlaine, in despair at losing him, shoots him with a revolver at the moment of departure (Brussels, July 10, 1873). They are separated, one in prison, the other at his mother's house.

Rimbaud draws up the balance: "Une Saison en Enfer" (April–August, 1873). He has been the dupe of his strength, of his devotion to men, of that literature which he now hates, for it has robbed him of solitude, inner strength, purity, and this to the profit of men whom he despises all, not having been able to save them. Rimbaud remains alone, face to God, henceforth the only object of interest, but he revolts against His domination. Between God and Rimbaud the conflict continues, for Rimbaud wants to create for himself alone, in himself alone, a spiritual universe whose master he would be, and which he would govern as he liked, organizing freely his thoughts, his sentiments and will.

Farmer in the Ardennes, teacher in England, student in Germany (1874–1875), vagabond in Italy, Dutch soldier in Sumatra, crimp on the Rhine, quarry boss in Cyprus (1879), circus hand in Copenhagen (1879), traveling salesman in the Gulf of Aden, exporter and geographer in Abyssinia (1880–1891), he struggles on, but each day his resources and hope diminish. At last everything is taken away. Stricken by an atrocious malady he loses piece by piece that body once powerful and beautiful. They have brought him back to Marseilles from Abyssinia. He knows he is going to die. Vanquished, he accepts his defeat. He confounds his irreducible world with that of God. He weeps, prays, confesses, communicates. His death comes on the tenth of November, 1891.

The very few works he left behind (only one was printed by himself: "Une Saison en Enfer", 1873) are the revelation of a new poetry. Instead of presenting in logical, metrical, imaginative form the world of ideas, sentiments and things, allowing only an occasional brief glimpse of the world of instincts and desires (as all earlier poetries had done), Rimbaud takes his stand in the inner world, he speaks of it and for it alone. The exterior is now evoked only by rare allusions. Hence those mysterious and profound visions, those flashes of light, that music come from afar, which are to be found, for example, in the "Bateau ivre."

Je sais les cieux crevant en éclairs, et les trombes
Et les ressacs et les courants; je sais le soir,
L'aube exaltée ainsi qu'un peuple de colombes,
Et j'ai vu quelquefois ce que l'homme a cru voir.

Rimbaud used all the rhythms, all the rhymes. He fractured eloquence, renewed images and comparisons, taught a new melody, and above all infused the whole with an immense ambition: the will to repulse the exterior world, as enemy, and as thing to overcome.

Then he stole away, leaving behind a strange, a marvelous adieu:

Arthur Rimbaud

DÉPART

Assez vu. La vision s'est rencontrée à tous les airs.
Assez eu. Rumeurs des villes, le soir, et au soleil, et
[*toujours.*
Assez connu. Les arrêts de la vie. — O Rumeurs et
[*Visions!*
Départ dans l'affection et les bruits neufs.

BOOKS

J. A. Rimbaud: "Oeuvres."

P. Berrichon: "Rimbaud, le poète" (*Mercure de France*).

M. Coulon: "Le problème de Rimbaud" (H. Goulet, depositary).

CHAPTER IV

VERLAINE

The Popular Poet of Symbolism

IN 1873 Rimbaud had retired, leaving Verlaine a great secret, a lesson of great price. He had revealed to him the fountain source of a new poetry.

Verlaine (1844–1896) was a greedy and malleable being; never was a man endowed with more senses, sentiments, desires and appetites. Flemish by his mother, Ardennais by his father, he was as sensual in soul as in body. He was devoured by an insatiable lust to feel and to be possessed. He had a certain amount of cunning, a measure of prudence, and judgment, but no will and no dignity. He begged all his life: money, pleasure, ideas, intoxication. His sole grandeur was a receptivity infinitely supple, direct, universal, perpetually attentive and tense.

Verlaine

His family, bourgeois, prosperous, came to
Paris when Verlaine was still a child. He was
a respectable student, and then an honest
employee in the offices of the Paris government (1854–1871). This job allowed him
leisure which he devoted to poetry. He
wrote Parnassian and Romantic poetry, like
everybody at that time, but with more talent
("Poèmes saturniens", 1866). He became engaged to a charming girl, like everybody, but
his fiancée was a little prettier, a little purer,
and much more unfortunate than is the or-
dinary lot of women. He was republican
and revolutionary with everybody under the
Empire, but he succeeded in compromising
himself more than the others during the Commune, under which he accepted the director-
ship of the press bureau.

Like all the poets of 1871 he was swept off
his feet by the precocious and astounding
genius of Rimbaud, but while the others
wondered and passed by, he abandoned himself to his domination, giving up wife, position
and poetry. Together, they traveled (England, Belgium, 1871–1873). The scandal was

such that his wife obtained a divorce, his friends disowned him, and the public condemned him. He made vain attempts to win back his wife, still keeping Rimbaud, which led, after the shooting at Brussels, to the prison of Mons, where he spent two years, calm, healthy, fruitful, the best of his life (1873–1875).

Verlaine was alone, deprived of everything. The prison separated him from the external world, but Rimbaud separated him from it even more, for this terrible friend had killed in him all taste for bourgeois and family life, and for art of the Romantic and Parnassian variety. "Poor Lélian" found himself truly simplified. Henceforth he would no longer be a bourgeois poet, but a poor man, a man of the crowds, of the soil, and of the highways. But Rimbaud had left him an infinite thirst for the enjoyment that is within, for spiritual satisfaction, for physical and moral enthusiasm pushed to the limits of delirium. Having reached this paroxysm, then abandoned, Verlaine could obtain succor only from God. Christ alone could offer him joys so intense, so dominating. Sincerely, and with fervor,

Verlaine was converted to Catholicism. He remained a believer to the end of his life, for his soul had need of abandon and intoxication as much as his body:

J'ai la fureur d'aimer. Mon coeur si faible est fou.

Never in French verse had been seen sensuality so insatiate, spirituality so sincere; dead for Verlaine are eloquence, rhetoric, elegance, decency, logic, everything which might come between him and his pleasures. As much as possible he reduces rhyme to simple assonance; of the poem he makes a song. His poetry swings on vague rhythms, on sweet and indefinite resonances, on furtive images, chatoyant, evocative, and so he defines his art of poetry:

> *Prends l'éloquence et tords-lui son cou!*
> *Tu feras bien, en train d'énergie,*
> *De rendre un peu la Rime assagie,*
> *Si l'on n'y veille, elle ira jusqu'où?*
>
> *De la musique encore et toujours!*
> *Que ton vers soit la chose envolée*
> *Qu'on sent qui fuit d'une âme en allée*
> *Vers d'autres cieux à d'autres amours.*

Like Rimbaud's, Verlaine's poetry is born in the subconscious, and there it remains, fleeing the outer world. But while the uncompromising Rimbaud had rejected all that failed to move the highest and most complex part of his being, Verlaine accepted everything. From this come his broad humanity, his popular character, and also the defects which are so irritating. In "Sagesse" (1881), an admirable poem of conversion, written under the literary influence of Rimbaud, the imperfections are hardly noticeable. But after 1884, when success had come, when Verlaine, too sure of himself, yielded to his weaknesses, and the sensual books appeared alternately with collections of religious poetry, his qualities sank gradually into confusion, grossness, stammering, just as his life was sinking into a vicious misery.

Once out of prison, Verlaine had at first led a respectable life as a teacher in a religious school at Rethel. Then he had abandoned himself to a violent passion for one of his students, Lucien Létinois, whom he adopted, and with whom he took up farming. Lucien's

death and the ruin of the agricultural venture
threw Verlaine back into teaching and literature. He returned to Paris and published
"Sagesse", which at first had no success whatever (1881).

His meeting with the publisher Vanier, who
was looking for a poet to launch, a new School
to serve and exploit, was the last stroke of luck
in Verlaine's life. In 1884 Vanier published
Verlaine's "Poètes Maudits", brief but striking sketches of Rimbaud, Corbière, and Mallarmé. This work, which depicted the poets
as infernal and sublime heroes, made a sharp
impression in artistic and poetic circles. In
his portrait of Rimbaud, Verlaine had put
all his emotion, his sorrow and desire. Thanks
to the legend of Rimbaud, harmoniously and
cleverly attached to Mallarmé, Corbière, etc.,
Verlaine in a single stroke founded a School,
the one which was given the name "decadent."
At first Verlaine consented to be its patron,
and celebrated "Decadence" in an admirable
sonnet:

Je suis l'Empire à la fin de la décadence,
Qui regarde passer les grands Barbares blancs

Since Victor Hugo

En composant des acrostiches indolents
D'un style d'or où la langueur du soleil danse.

But he let it die without regret, and rallied to the sister and rival school, which, since 1886, has gone under the incorrect but elegant name of "Symbolism."

Young men began to crowd around Verlaine. They were tired of the god Hugo, and could not feel at home with the Parnassians, stiff, timorous, forever aloof. Verlaine on the contrary was free, the man who dragged at random through hospitals, dives, and in the gutters. This ragamuffin in love with everything, this tramp who never rested, this inspired and miserable poet, who had pushed all things too far, and preserved of grandeur only his refusal to settle down, and an unquenchable thirst for alcohol, women and the mystical life, this happy and crafty maniac was bound to fascinate the youth. In Paris everything Bohemian, adventurous, daring, went mad over him. They did not take him for the leader of a School, or for a master, but for this they loved him the more, and abandoned themselves the more spontaneously to their admiration. Verlaine could arouse neither jealousy nor fear.

He published his verses: "Jadis et Naguère" (1885), "Parallèlement" (1889), "Bonheur" (1891), "Liturgies intimes" (1892), "Odes en son honneur" (1893), "Epigrammes" (1894), "Invectives" (1896), and let the Symbolist School grow with indifference. Being asked by Jules Huret what the Symbolists were, Verlaine replied "Cymbalists" and turned his back. He ridiculed the more ardent of the Symbolist theorists, and got amusement out of the quarrels between René Ghil and Moréas. Toward the end of his life nothing could interest him but a few women, with whom he lived, drink, and the memory of Rimbaud, which haunted him invincibly. In 1891 he told Retté, who had come to see him at the hospital, "Since Arthur Rimbaud's death I see him every night. I cannot accept that death. Years had passed since we had seen one another, but Rimbaud, his art and his face, were always shining in the depths of my spirit. . . . For me Rimbaud is an ever living reality, a sun which flames in me, and will not be extinguished. . . ."

Verlaine wandered, drunk or haggard, never alone, never attentive. He was seeking still. He was always in search of something, of some one, and especially of him who had carried away with him the most bitter pleasures. He could not forget the old compact, the journeys, the intoxication of the roads. Judging his disciples too careful of the things of this world, too anxious to define, to stop, to shut themselves up in a doctrine and a group, he desired especially to disappear. Death brought him comfort in 1896, and this great poet, the only popular poet of Symbolism, had a fine funeral, with speeches, like M. Hugo.

BOOKS

P. Verlaine: "Les Poètes Maudits."
"Sagesse."
"Jadis et Naguère."
E. Lepelletier: "P. Verlaine."

CHAPTER V

STEPHANE MALLARME

The Theorist of Intellectual Symbolism

BETWEEN the hard life of a Rimbaud and
the hiccuping existence of a Verlaine, Stéphane
Mallarmé's life is straight, single, and white,
like the vocation of a monk.

Mallarmé was born in 1842, of a distinguished family, who brought him up with care.
He lost his mother when still a child, but the
affection of his grandmother softened his first
years. Even then he dreamt of poetry, and
on meeting the works of Poe he hesitated no
longer; he decided to abandon his family and
work out his own destiny. Married very
young to a woman whom he loved greatly,
and of whom he spoke with profound and
respectful tenderness, he had to have some
means of earning a living: he learned English
and became a teacher of that language in the

41

state schools. After some years in the provinces he got a place in Paris. He was first at the lycée Condorcet, then at Janson-de-Sailly, finally at Rollin. He performed this monotonous and wearying duty conscientiously, but without joy. He passed his happy moments in his family, with his wife and daughter, whom he loved equally, among his friends, or before his desk laden with white paper, which he blackened with discretion. He sacrificed as little time as possible and as little strength to the necessities and to pleasure. He lived outside of those things, within himself. His house and his family served him as a wall. "I wander little", he said to Verlaine in 1885, "preferring above everything, in an apartment defended by my family, to dwell among a few old and rare possessions, and the sheet of paper frequently white."

He lived for his thought and his friends.

He received on Tuesday evenings. And after 1885 (when Verlaine and Huysmans had attracted public attention to him, and when the Symbolist School had recognized him as one of their guides) his Tuesdays were much frequented. Don't imagine either a fête or a "salon!" He received in his dining room, which was a modest room, and very fine (eighteenth century furniture, two pictures by Berthe Morizot, a Manet, a Monet, a Redon and a cast by Rodin).

On entering, a great silence met the visitor, giving pause to life, stifling the noises from outside, and the solicitous, delicate friendship of Mallarmé greeted him immediately. They sat around the table. Mallarmé would smoke his little short pipe, seated in his rocking-chair or leaning against the mantel. They spoke slowly, interested above all in listening to the master, eager to learn, rather than to display themselves. Mallarmé's learned, strange, brilliant discourses unfolded like a story, interrupted like the psalms by long pauses. Then Mlle. Mallarmé would enter, bringing the punch. And they drank discreetly before separating. Mallarmé's Tuesdays were not meant for conversation, but for a sort of spoken meditation, in which visitors played the rôle of stimulators, disciples, audience, but not interlocutors. He alone "celebrated the office", for in all this there was something religious, grand, touching, childish, as in everything which is very pure. Mallarmé spoke well, and, willing or not, his hearers submitted to his charm. It is said that a journalist who came to hear him one day was so enthusiastic over his remarks that he begged him to send him a ccpy of them immediately. "I must arrange them a little", said Mallarmé, who several weeks later sent the good man a few sheets of paper of which he recognized nothing and understood not a word. Mallarmé had "styled" his words, a work to which he attached infinite importance, but which embarrassed the more superficial of his admirers.

It was at Mallarmé's Tuesdays that was formed the élite of the young literary generation of 1890–1900: Claudel, André Gide, Régnier, Viélé-Griffin, Mockel, P. Louys, P. Valéry, etc. Also, Rue de Rome, could be seen Villiers de l'Isle-Adam, a noble soul, lofty, pure, and who then passed as a "master of prose", the painter Whistler, whose biting wit and generous friendship were equally precious to Mallarmé, and C. Mendès, whose presence in this company is as surprising as the very real influence which he exercised everywhere at that time, even among the Symbolists.

Mallarmé knew how to reconcile all these incongruous elements. He was passionately fond of music, and had a profound comprehension, which was then unusual, of painting; he listened to Mendès, admired Villiers, and took an interest in everything done by Hugo and Zola.

Thus lived this man, an exile in his own age, of which he said: "At bottom I consider the contemporary epoch an interregnum for the poet, who had best keep clear of it, for it is too decrepit, and too much in preparatory effervescence for him to do anything except work in mystery, in view of the future, or of never at all, and from time to time send his visiting card, stanzas or sonnets, to the living, to avoid being stoned by them, should they by chance suspect that they do not exist." These "visiting cards" are the admirable "Après-midi d'un faune", which got him into trouble with his first friends the Parnassians (1876), his poems, printed (forty-seven copies) in 1887, his "Pages" (1891), "Vers et Prose" (the most complete of the collections published by him, 1893), "Divagations" (1897). He had also done excellent translations of Poe (in 1875, 1888), of Beckford, of Whistler, and contributed to a good number of little Symbolist reviews.

Like his conversations, each one of his works was an essay, an attempt, rather than an achievement in his eyes. Mallarmé's object would have been to found a pure poetry, beyond the reach of interests or low passions, and capable of arousing æsthetic pleasure alone, without admixture. He was seeking always a poetry entirely disinterested and abstract. His progress lies in the discovery of new means of decanting his poetry, of separating it further from the world. Above all he attacked the word, and he would have liked to see the creation of words uniquely poetical. To this end he resorted to the use of rare, technical, or ancient terms, or else employed the usual vocables in their etymological sense,

or with oblique meanings. For him, words
were not simple signs comparable to pieces of
money which are exchanged while remaining
themselves unmodified, but allegories, which
take on a peculiar value for every different
person. He did not use punctuation to mark
the stops fixed by grammar and logic, but
rather the pauses which his thought and sentiment had chosen. He did not group words
according to grammar or logic, but suppress-
ing personal pronouns, verbs, prepositions
and adverbs, transforming epithets so as to
set them in relief, he sought unity not in
the phrase, but in the verse: a new and
supple frame, harmony formed by words
which thought and desire have brought
together.

He respects the cesura and rhyme, solicits
alliteration, and invents marvelous images,
subtle, distant, infinitely rich, for he knows
how to evoke impressions of all the senses,
and to combine them.

When he says, for example, in one of his
most beautiful sonnets:

Since Victor Hugo

Le vierge, le vivace et le bel aujourd'hui
Va-t-il nous déchirer avec un coup d'aile ivre,
Ce lac dur oublié que hante sous le givre
Le transparent glacier des vols qui n'ont pas fui!

Un cygne d'autrefois . . .

he is thinking of the poet whose desires and
efforts have not been able to take their flight
at the proper time (*les vols qui n'ont pas fui*),
and have remained prisoned in the frosts of
weariness, under the ice of time, cold, mate-
rialistic, cruel. In his eyes there is no hope for
the poet except in a sudden and hardly prob-
able explosion, an abrupt reversal of the future, of that mysterious to-day, which is still
virgin (*vierge*), for it has not been soiled by
the actions and wiles of man, which has long
to live (*vivace*), for it is just being born, and
is beautiful (*bel*) with all the hope which it
awakens. The high, clear idea held in this
quatrain transpierces images and comparisons
which move simultaneously the senses of sight
and touch, creating perceptions of hardness,
cold, and movement. The first two verses roll
rapidly on the carefully placed "v's", while,

on the contrary, the "i's" of the rhyme seem
to compress and harden the poem. The comma
which follows the second verse, in a place
where the sense would not allow a stop, indi-
cates that voice and thought, having attained a summit, should remain for an instant
suspended.

This too brief analysis will give a notion of
the superhuman but fruitful effort which
Mallarmé imposed upon himself. Each one
of his poems is thus an impossible venture in
the direction of the absolute. In truth these
ventures are always vain, for whatever is
produced by man in a burst of desperate energy, ends by suffering in some measure the
domination of time, circumstance, the social
group, of pitiless chance, which will not toler-
ate perfection and freedom. But every poem
we write is a game played against this chance,
a cast of the dice to obtain a combination perfect, and in its way eternal. This is what
Mallarmé said in his last work: "Un coup
de dé jamais n'abolira le hasard", where he
attempts to express the idea not only by
sounds, the sense of the syllables, and images,

but also by the position of the characters on the page, and the relation between the white and the black.

This was his last and most daring attempt. In the fall of 1898 he died suddenly, and silently. He was the last of the great Symbolists, the noblest, perhaps, in his pride and his sadness, the most sorrowful too, for he had neither Rimbaud's wrath nor Verlaine's drunkenness to console him, and he constantly measured the distance between his ambition and his accomplishment. His humility, his courtesy, his resignation, his marriage even, conceal a suffering which terrifies, but through which his works are vivified, even to-day.

BOOKS

S. Mallarmé: "Vers et prose" (1893).
A. Mockel: "S. Mallarmé" (1899).
A. Thibaudet: "La poésie de S. Mallarmé" (1912).

CHAPTER VI

THE SYMBOLIST SCHOOL

or The Last Crusade

WHILE Rimbaud, Verlaine, and Mallarmé were blazing new trails for our poetry, part of the public abandoned the reigning Schools, Parnasse and Naturalism, whose antichristian philosophy and materialism had aroused considerable opposition, particularly in the bourgeois classes. At the same time certain of the younger generation declared themselves weary of a formal poetry and a declamatory and social prose. The "Bohemians" gathered in cafés, organized clubs: Hydropathes, Zutistes, Decadents, etc. (1880 to 1884). They recited Baudelaire, applauded Rollinat, and demanded freedom for poetry.

These vague tendencies took form about 1884. At that date Verlaine published at Vanier's a curious and fascinating volume, immediately famous, on certain poets whom he dubbed "accursed" and who gave the impression of being new. A Naturalistic novelist, Huysmans, published a meretricious but striking tale of the life of an æsthete enamored of the "accursed" and proclaiming himself their disciple. Finally, two writers of talent — Bauclaire and Vicaire — amused themselves by composing a rather harsh satire, but very funny, on the "decadents": "Les Déliquescences d'Adoré Floupette." This volume delighted the general public and excited innumerable discussions; some went so far as to consider it authentic. In this book, Adoré Floupette, decadent poet, published his complete works, and his friend the druggist-poet, Tapora, described the fatiguing and heroic existence of his beloved Adoré. There were verses like the following, parody of Verlaine:

> *Ah! comme verte s'en alla*
> *Par la porte à peine entr'ouverte*
> *Mon âme effroyablement verte*
> *Dans l'azur vert de ce jour-là!*

The newcomers were thus presented to the public in a nimbus of ridicule, but also of

strangeness and glory. Verlaine was the
drunkard and mystic, and Rimbaud king
of a Negro island. The great papers engaged in acrimonious discussions (campaigns
of P. Arène in *Gil Blas*, May, 1885, of Suter
Laumann in *Justice*, June, 1885, of Paul Bourde
and then Anatole France in the *Temps*, 1885–
1886). This all attracted attention, and the
younger generation came in, attracted by
danger, novelty, and the scandal.

A number of groups were formed, the first
the Decadent School (1885), of which Verlaine consented to be a member, and which
was directed by the good Anatole Baju, "*cet
Anatole si Baju*", according to Tailhade. This
excellent fellow, son of a miller, schoolteacher
by profession and litterateur by apostolic zeal,
founded with a few friends the review *Le Dé-
cadent*, which had its happy days. Unfortu-
nately Baju was too rustic and too naïve. He
published, without turning a hair, false poems
by Rimbaud and apocryphal odes by General
Boulanger. He was ridiculed and supplanted
by other champions, who were craftier and
more sedate. "Decadence" gave way to Sym-

bolism. This term, furthermore, was better suited to those who desired respectability and social success.

It had been revealed to the public by Jean Moréas (Papadiamantopoulos, by his real name), a young Greek who had come to France to seek his fortune, and whom Barrès described at that time as "an old gentleman of the Peloponnesus." Moréas had all the qualities of a leader — decision, strength, ambition; he was also an elegant poet and endowed with remarkable musical sense. He was the first (1886) to get a Symbolist manifesto accepted by a great paper (*le Figaro*). At the same time G. Kahn (author of the "Palais Nomades") felt within him the vocation of the great man. He had an original theory which he desired to impose as something more advanced than the doctrines of Verlaine, Rimbaud, and Mallarmé: free verse, a verse without rhyme, cesura, capitals, or fixed meter, fashioned only by the intuition of the poet. He loved to direct reviews, but did not know how to keep them from dying (*le Symboliste, la Vogue,* 1886).

A rival of Moréas and Kahn, R. Ghil, aspired to the laurels of Imperator and founded a School, "the Symbolist and Harmonist Group", subsequently known by the name of "Groupe Philosophico-instrumentiste." Ghil evolved out of Symbolism a scientific poetry based upon the exact correspondence of sounds and colors. Verlaine assured him in vain that his theory was stupid; Ghil would not believe it. He persisted until his disciples and his ideas were worn away.

But living and working in solitude, more deserving of a leader's place, though fated to an early death, was a charming spirit, Jules Laforgue. He was at that time reader to the Empress of Germany at Berlin, where he wrote his "Complaintes", verses inexpressibly melodious, and of a harsh sadness which is surprising in a being so young and so gifted, and also his "Moralités Légendaires", astonishing tales in prose, full of sarcasm, imagination, and power. Laforgue was one of the creators of Symbolist prose; he invented a language which was at the same time refined and popular, supple and brutal. For this reason his name ought to remain. The *Vogue* published his "Moralités" in 1886, and as he died immediately afterward, he was chosen by the Symbolists as one of their masters.

All of these efforts, these discussions, interested the crowd. In 1888 an article by Brunetière, hardly perspicacious, but generous, in the *Revue des Deux Mondes*, praised these young poets who were trying to escape from Naturalism, and won them a few friends in Catholic circles. Some of the Parnassians joined them, and the favor of the public inclined toward the amusing innovators. Moréas in 1891 had the satisfaction of seeing himself extolled by the very persons who had formerly attacked him, Anatole France in particular. All the writers flocked to the Symbolist dinners and soirées; Zola himself appeared, curious to mingle with these revolutionists of literature. The School had a doctrine, a theater (P. Fort's Théâtre d'Art, 1890), substantial reviews (*la Plume*, 1889, the *Mercure de France*, 1890, the *Revue Blanche*, 1891, which was especially useful for its editions of the Symbolist poets). Its hour seemed to have come.

But success killed it. Moréas, the principal artisan of the victory, was the first to desert (1891). For him Symbolism had been only a means to surpass Naturalism and Romanticism. His character and his gifts impelled him toward a serious poetry, with clear, sharp lines and measured tones. He founded the Romanic School, which aimed to reëstablish classical traditions, and wrote his "Stances" (1898–1901), which contain accents that compel admiration:

Quand je viendrai m'asseoir dans le vent, dans la nuit,
Au bout du rocher solitaire,
Quand je n'entendrai plus, en t'écoutant, le bruit
Que fait mon cœur sur cette terre,

Ne te contente pas, Océan, de jeter
Sur mon visage un peu d'écume:
D'un coup de lame alors il te faut m'emporter
Pour dormir dans ton amertume.

Symbolism could not survive the defection of Moréas, who was the most serious of its champions. To be sure, two great reviews, the *Mercure* (founded by M. Vallette) and the *Revue Blanche* (the Natanson brothers) continued as centers of Symbolism. But it was no longer the original and pure doctrine of Verlaine, Rimbaud, Mallarmé. The *Mercure* had welcomed writers of all kinds (Renard, Gourmont, Tailhade, L. Dumur, etc.). Gourmont, its best critic, despised Rimbaud as much as he misunderstood him. The Symbolism of the *Mercure* was above all emancipation; it had lost the lofty spiritual ambitions which in the beginning had animated the heroes of Symbolism. And so too with the *Revue Blanche*, where a great deal of attention was paid to social questions, to anarchy.

The Symbolist School had been a misunderstanding. These young men enamored of Verlaine, enthusiastic over Rimbaud and Mallarmé, had failed to perceive that their masters were proposing a crusade, a "chasse spirituelle." They had written books and tried to found Schools, when the real need was to work on themselves. Symbolism should have been a kind of religion. It required too much effort, too much concentration and devotion to last as a literary group. Far from exhausting the ideas of Rimbaud and Mallarmé, the Symbolist School had passed them by, sealing thus their own fate, and bequeathing to future generations the true treasures of Symbolism, by them to be discovered and brought to fruition. Unconsciously, then, they were protecting the future at their own expense. After 1900 nothing was left but a mysterious ambition unknown to the general public, and a few literary theories, hardly coherent, hardly logical, but full of promise.

Through the Symbolists the crowd had acquired an interest in the "subconscious", and a taste for the fabulous; the old verse forms had been made flexible, and a new one, entirely intuitive, had been created. Music had been taught the poets, the musicians, and the philosophers, and thus the way made clear for Bergson and Debussy.

A whole district of France had had revealed its true sensibility, which the earlier Schools had neither discovered nor expressed. Symbolism is a poetry of the North. It was born in the Ardennes and in Flanders. There the flame which it lit is still burning. Maurice

Maeterlinck is the most glorious interpreter of this popular Symbolism. Playwright ("La princesse Maleine", 1889), philosopher ("Trésor des Humbles", 1896) and poet ("Douze Chansons", 1896), it costs him no effort to abandon himself to the obscure forces of the personality, deliberately renouncing the lucid intelligence. The new doctrine corresponds to his most secret and most profound aspirations. If his theology seems hollow, and his prose heavy and sometimes formless, his poetical babblings are marvelous. Better than any one else he has evoked the lasting, unconquerable element of Symbolism, that search for the absolute, that tireless quest for beauty free, pure, and of within.

> *J'ai cherché trente ans, mes sœurs,*
> *Où s'est-il caché?*
> *J'ai marché trente ans, mes sœurs,*
> *Sans m'en rapprocher ...*
>
> *J'ai marché trente ans, mes sœurs,*
> *Et mes pieds sont las,*
> *Il était partout, mes sœurs,*
> *Et n'existe pas ...*

L'heure est triste enfin, mes sœurs,
Otez vos sandales,
Le soir meurt aussi, mes sœurs,
Et mon âme a mal . . .

Vous avez seize ans, mes sœurs,
Allez loin d'ici,
Prenez mon bourdon, mes sœurs,
Et cherchez aussi . . .

BOOKS

A. Barré: "Le Symbolisme", 1911. (A book which might be excellent, but contains a great many errors and should be revised. Out of print.)

G. Kahn: "Symbolistes et Décadents", (1902).

Retté: "Le Symbolisme", (1903).

R. de Gourmont: "Souvenirs du Symbolisme." (*Promenades littéraires*, 2e série, 1906.)

CHAPTER VII

FROM M. RENAN TO M. TAINE

or The Demon of Scientific Certitude

FRENCH prose has always been a social instrument. It has followed the political and economic transformations of the country. Comparable to money, it is a medium of exchange, and like money, requires stability and clarity to fulfill its function. It places lucidity higher than the picturesque, or variety or suppleness. The Frenchman will not be fooled; he thinks he understands his neighbor and the things that surround him. He believes that everything can be made intelligible to everybody, if only you know how to go about it. This requirement has dominated our prose literature since Rabelais and Montaigne. Still, the passing of the centuries has altered its character. Not to be a fool in the seventeenth century, it was enough to understand clearly. (I think, hence I exist.) In the eighteenth century, good reasons were demanded. In the nineteenth it was tangible evidence. Since the era of experimentation and the discovery of new forms of life (industry), the prestige of science has become so great that everything must be demonstrated to the senses as well as to the mind. Detailed explanations are insisted upon, from men, from things, and from Him who made them. We are no longer satisfied with the logical definition, but demand a coherent certitude, founded upon physical impressions as well as reasoning. Thus new sentiments have entered the soul of the Frenchman, while others have been weakened. Science has taught us pleasures hitherto unknown, and especially the pleasure of possessing objects by all the senses, the imagination, and the intellect. This delight has become a sort of intoxication. It has finally prevailed in all domains, even those which would seem to be farthest removed from science. And our prose has not escaped.

Two men in the second half of the nineteenth century insured the triumph of the Demon of Scientific Certitude in French literature: Renan and Taine, very unlike in talent, character, taste, but great men both, and inspired.

I should like first to depict the disquieting figure of M. Renan: that great mass of soft white flesh, lit by little eyes, gleaming and dangerous, will o' the wisp of the swamp, that heavy body devoid of muscles, but tissue of nerves so delicate that no one would venture to jostle it, and that joy of the whole being expanded by prayer — or possibly by the digestion. I should like to describe a life made up of fortunate devotions and rewarded sacrifices. Of humble origin, M. Renan (1823–1892) was at first a seminarist. But he lost his faith before ordination and did not hesitate to abandon the holy house where he was beloved by everybody, and to enter the world, where he was without resources and without protection. Nevertheless, at the end of twelve years (1845–1857), he was an *agrégé de philosophie, docteur ès lettres*, member of the Academy of Inscriptions (at thirty-three) and famous for the fluid and charming style of his works, for his marvelous erudition, and for his politely hostile attitude toward the Catholic Church. (In 1856 M. Renan had married.)

The Second Empire brought him world-wide renown. The Government cherished and at first protected him, sending him on an archeological expedition to Syria (1860–1861) and appointing him professor at the Collège de France. Then came a conflict with the Minister of Public Instruction, because M. Renan had declared from his chair at the Collège de France that he no longer believed in the divinity of Christ. Renan was removed (1864), but the tremendous, scandalous, and triumphant success of the "Vie de Jésus" relieved him of all material care. He devoted his leisure to erudition ("Histoire des Origines du Christianisme", 1866 to 1883) but at the same time allowing himself other researches and profane digressions. The Revolution of 1870 gave him back his chair at the Collège de France, and the Republic, generously pardoning his monarchical tendencies and his

contempt for the vulgar, honored him in every
way. He replied to the favors of fortune by
a series of works on the "Histoire du Peuple
d'Israël" (1888–1894), a few fantasies which
consoled his old age for the privations of his
youth ("Abbesse de Jouarre", 1886), and his
marvelous "Souvenirs d'Enfance et de Jeunesse" (1893). Death took him gently on the
heights of glory.

He had sacrificed everything to science,
but science had paid him well. M. Renan
bequeathed to future generations a complex
doctrine, full of reticences and insinuations,
shrouded in clouds of changing hue, but the
sun which shone in its center was Science. In
his great work ("Histoire du Christianisme"),
M. Renan had shown how the most august of
religions had been born, and in composing this
book he had rejected all idea of mystery, holding worthless every fact which could not be
explained on scientific grounds. M. Renan
had taught that man must turn his soul
toward the Ideal, but that this ideal should
be Truth; and in his eyes only Science could
attain certitude. "Would to God", he cried,

"that I might bring a few beautiful souls to the understanding that in the pure cult of the human faculties and in the divine objects which they attain there is a religion as suave, as rich in delights, as the most venerable of cults. Science and humanism afford sufficient religious nourishment." ("Avenir de la Science", page 318.) According to Renan, Science ought gradually to take the place of religion, not destroying it, but voiding it of its dogmatic content and preserving the rest: ideal aspiration, charity, morality, voluptuousness of the soul.

Renan's genius consists in a subtle and greedy intelligence which refused to renounce the enjoyment of the very thing which it was criticizing and destroying. Attacking Catholicism, he still kept everything which Catholicism had given him, taught him, and confided to him. This very ambiguity made him the most redoubtable of enemies for the Church, for it grouped around him all the disciples of mystic dilettantism (very stylish between 1880 and 1900), who liked to extract subtle pleasures from religions in which they no longer

believed; the polite anticlericals, who desired
to keep on good terms with their opponents;
and desperate believers, who still loved and
respected the faith from which they were
breaking away.

M. Renan's extraordinary comprehension
and his multifarious sensibility gave him
enormous prestige, which the years have not
destroyed. His style may appear whitish and
often affected (for example the famous prayer
on the Acropolis), his thought too clever, and
his mysticism sanctimonious, but no one before had given so lofty or so complex an image
of the scientific ideal, irresistible for the mind,
and so seductive for the flesh.

M. Taine (1828–1893) is little and dry com-
pared with M. Renan. His reputation rested
upon his ability to draw correct conclusions,
teach clearly, and also his real moral worth.
He vulgarized and applied to literature the
ideas which his illustrious predecessor had in-
troduced into the religiosity of the century.
Like Renan, Taine knew no joy above that
of scientific certitude; he would have made
it the supreme goal of artists and writers. At

the foundation of everything is the fact, the "little true fact", observed impartially, and classified according to its intrinsic characteristics. Facts, collected and interpreted, constitute psychology, the only branch of philosophy which seemed scientific to Taine; facts give value to history, for history also ought to be a science, turned toward the study of man's past; facts, again, guide the novelist and the dramatist. Indeed, according to Taine, "what historians do for the past, the great novelists and dramatists do for the present." Every work of art is thus a material product, the result of the working of natural forces. A book or a poem can be explained by the "point in time", the "environment" and the "race." In it can be discovered the action of these three forces, and it can be interpreted like a problem in mechanics. Literature thus takes on a precision which formerly belonged only to mathematics and geometry. And Taine, having reached the goal, looks back and contemplates the clear, coherent and simple synthesis which he has created. To tell the truth, this contemplation was not without bitterness. If Taine had a mediocre artistic sense, he had been endowed with an exacting conscience, and the very realization of his success terrified him. He suffered, not like Renan, voluptuously melancholy at having killed his God, but with gall and humiliation, miserable at not being able to love, perceive, or even doubt that unknowable which was so real for others.

This grief, nobly borne, did not lessen the influence of his work. Taine had encased his ideas in a sonorous and solid covering; his prose, constructed according to the best traditional rhetoric, made a fine showing. His noble character, his social zeal, and his naïveté were there mirrored as in a glass. It was very popular. From 1880 to 1910 M. Taine was the master of the serious youth of the country, who took from him their conception of history, literary criticism, and the novel.

Thus did scientific certitude establish its empire over French prose, thanks to the genius of M. Renan and the respectability of M. Taine.

BOOKS

Renan: "Souvenirs d'Enfance et de Jeunesse."

Taine: "Les Origines de la France contemporaine."

G. Séailles: "Renan."

Victor Giraud: "Essai sur Taine."

CHAPTER VIII

EMILE ZOLA AND NATURALISM

BETWEEN 1830 and 1900 science was kind and benignant in France. It made a great many people rich and killed very few. One whole class owed to science its fortune, its rise, and its prestige: the engineers, the foremen, the doctors, the schoolteachers, the pharmacists, etc. And it was precisely this hard-working and educated lower middle class that supported the July Monarchy and then the Second Empire. It was this class, finally, which in 1870 took the power in person with M. Thiers, M. Gambetta, and the Third Republic. At first there were a few disputes as to which middle-class group was going to govern: but it finally became evident that the "upper middle class" would have to lower their colors to their humbler brothers who, in closer contact with the people of the towns and the country were better situated to handle the electoral instrument (or the elector). They took the power; they also made themselves a literature, and of course paid back to science what science had given them. For centuries, even before winning ease and authority, they had possessed a noisy, corpulent prose, enamored of the objects of physical life, with a penchant toward satire, and animated by a tireless optimism, badly concealed behind resounding and fleshy words. Rabelais, Furetière, Charles Sorel, Diderot, Restif de la Bretonne are in this line, and should be looked upon as the ancestors of Naturalism.

Nevertheless this doctrine owes its success and even its name to Zola, who incarnated the tendencies and the principal characteristics of this class. French by his mother, Italian by his father, he had been endowed with neither brilliance, nor beauty, nor fortune, but with extraordinary assiduity, a great deal of ambition, and an excitable sensuality which left untouched his rather meager sensibility. His bringing-up was his own work. His father, after many attempts and failures, had finished as an engineer by achieving something great, the Aix canal; but a sudden death overtook him in the midst of this work, and the Zola family had to struggle bitterly to avoid falling back into the people.

Emile Zola, who had been a good student at Aix, was a bad one in Paris, and failed his *baccalauréat*. He had to work for a living and became a clerk in the publishing house of Hachette. But he did not admit defeat: undiscouraged, he wrote deplorable verse. He drafted uninspired short stories. He contributed to the papers (*Figaro, Evénement, Vie parisienne, Petit Journal, Tribune,* etc.). From 1859 to 1866 his life was hard. It was his art criticism that first attracted attention. ("Mes haines", 1864–1865.) But he was neither adroit nor amusing, and the higher middle-class journals could find no use for his talents. "Thérèse Raquin" had a certain success, after which Zola married. He was on the road to finish as a "novelist of repute" when the War of 1870 came on, transforming the public, raising Zola immediately to the governing class (he was almost a *sous-préfet*), placing his ideas among the popular tendencies, and giving a brusque stimulus to his genius. Destiny, kind at last, furnished him a priceless friend in the person of Charpentier, a clever and daring young book dealer who became his publisher, secured him first his daily bread, then ease, finally wealth, and scattered his great novels through the world.

It was then that Zola invented, founded, and imposed Naturalism. Adopting the ideas of Taine, applying those of Claude Bernard to literature, following, so he believed, the techniques of Stendhal, Balzac, and Duranty, he proclaimed that the novel should be "experimental", that it should give for the life of society the same kind of data that biology furnishes for the world of living beings. "To-day the novel has become the tool of the century, the great inquest on man and nature." ("Romanciers naturalistes", p. 331.) Every novel should be conceived and prepared like a scientific experiment. It should be written, built as a complete and impartial statement. Thus the novel attained that scientific certitude so dear to M. Taine and to all the serious minds of the century. Zola wanted it also sonorous, popular, and psychological; he owed that to his class, his education, and his instincts.

The doctrine thus defined he applied honestly. He collected notes on the principal events of his time, out of which he made novels. The whole constitutes the great Naturalistic epic of the "Rougon-Macquart" (1871–1895), a scientific and lyrical tale of the life of a French bourgeois family of the nineteenth century. The books in which he described the existence of the miners ("Germinal", 1885), the ravages of alcohol ("l'Assommoir", 1876), the War of 1870 ("la Débâcle", 1892), were a tremendous sensation. (In 1907, two hundred and eighteen thousand copies of "la Débâcle" had been sold, two hundred and four thousand of "Nana", one hundred and fifty-seven thousand of "l'Assommoir.") In spite of protests and clamors from the critics, the epoch rocognized itself. Zola had founded a School: the group of Médan (from the name of Zola's country estate). Hennique, Céard, P. Alexis, Huysmans, Maupassant declared themselves disciples. From 1880 to 1890 he reigned.

He was not naturally an observer. He had to stare at a thing to see it. He was not an agreeable writer. His style was heavy and at times incorrect. He lacked psychological sense and constructive imagination. He had very little taste, and an uneven culture. But his furious industry, tireless will, the horror and admiration which the masses inspired in him, into whose midst he had come so near falling and dying engulfed, his comprehension of crowds, of bodies, his verbal lyricism — all this made him a powerful writer. His descriptions of failures and soiled lives, where he put all his sincerity, all the terror which such disasters aroused in him, shocked and overwhelmed his age, but they left no one unmoved, and there Zola had genius.

Naturalism triumphed with him, with Maupassant, with Daudet (although the latter kept aloof from the Médan group). Daudet (1840–1897), more moderate, more cultivated, and endowed with a more perceptive soul, had adapted Naturalism to the French tradi-

tionalist circles. Like Zola's, his novels are
social and documentary, but he uses less science, and is more solicitous of literary tone.
Like Zola, Daudet pleased because of his
pictures of the lower classes, and for the thrill
which the thankful bourgeois felt in reading
him: "What miseries we have escaped!"
Strictly speaking, neither Zola nor Daudet
was of the people (laborers and peasants);
hence they spoke of them in moving and convincing fashion, one tragically, the other with
emotion and pity.

Maupassant (1850–1893) employed hard
contempt. He was the most gifted of the
great Naturalists, and might have been the
most original. But he had need of poetry,
beauty, luxury, and he was ill at ease in the
doctrine which he practiced. The literary
asceticism which he imposed upon himself was
a torture. Nevertheless, his works were received with enthusiasm, and his reputation
is still immense outside of France. That is
just, for Maupassant, by encasing Naturalism
in a severe and exact style, and by expressing
it in short stories, had eliminated the two

principal obstacles to the diffusion of the new
literature: the tedium emanating from the
thick volumes, and the contempt in which
they were held by the "connoisseurs." (In
the domain of arts and letters, human respect
is a despotic force. "Especially in France",
Stendhal would say.)

The triumph of Naturalism was complete;
people said "Hugo and Zola." Maupassant
became a classic, and the school children were
given the "Lettres de mon Moulin" as a perfect model of French. Outside of France
Naturalism established a crude and sometimes
disagreeable impression of our country. For-
eigners took to admiring our vices and our
genius. In their opinion France was at last
reconciled to herself, and, as under Louis XIV,
possessed a literature in harmony with her
political and social régime. French literature,
until then the most hierarchized in the world,
seemed about to open its doors to everybody,
to place itself within the reach of everybody, and to abandon the old ideas of rule,
style, decorum, complicated courtesy, and
subtle psychology.

That was not so. Naturalism was a flash in the pan. As early as 1890 it was in difficulties. The higher classes, the intellectuals, found it wearying; they ridiculed its scientific pretensions. The subconscious and religiosity had been made fashionable by the Symbolists. In vain Zola told the Symbolists, "I will do what you are trying to do", and plunged into a sort of social mysticism (the Dreyfus affair and Zola's last books: "les Quatre Evangiles"), men began not to listen and to cease buying his books. Huysmans went over to the enemy. At last Daudet's death in 1897 and Zola's (1902) brought the Naturalist era to a close.

Despite talent or genius, the Naturalists had not been able to impose their tastes upon the higher classes, and these classes in France have kept the privilege of being the regulators and the conservers of literature. On the whole the scientific religion was distasteful to them for its verbal and superficial qualities; Zola's experimentation they considered arbitrary and ridiculous. Finally, we, as a nation, are inclined to take small interest in the crowd, and our individualism would soon have eliminated the Naturalists as a dominating group. But the instincts which formed that doctrine and that School are still living forces: great writers have remained faithful to them. Among these, Jules Renard should be mentioned first of all, and, on another plane, Mirbeau.

Naturalism was a brief episode in our literary history, but it left behind a few good books, and it gave a hearing to one of the most laborious and respectable classes of the French nation.

BOOKS

Lepelletier: "Emile Zola."

Deffoux and Zavie: "Le groupe de Médan.

H. Massis: "Comment Zola composait ses romans" (which seems to me an excellent book and most "judicious").

Zola: "Germinal", etc.

CHAPTER IX

M. ANATOLE FRANCE

The Master of Official Literature in France

IN 1909 the Symbolist and Naturalist Schools were dead. They had disappeared without satisfying the tendencies responsible for their being, and without involving those tendencies in their ruin. The Symbolist doctrine and Naturalism continued to dominate distinguished minds, furnishing themes for research and working instruments, but no longer commanded an exclusive cult. In fact, the functioning of the republican and democratic régime, the constant electoral struggle since 1870, had finally brought an influence to bear on French literature and especially the prose. By 1895–1900 the young writers had ceased to be disinterested and abstract dreamers; they all wanted to be heard by the crowd, to be elected, or at least applauded.

Barrès was a candidate for political office. Jaurès, Zola, Péguy, France battled for Captain Dreyfus, while Barrès, Bourget, Maurras, Coppée, Lemaître went down into the arena to defend the cause of the army and nationalism. The Dreyfus affair was the incident which revealed to all their vocation as social and political apostles, but they would have got there sooner or later, for such was the taste of the times. They had no intention of denying either M. Taine or M. Renan, or the cult of science, but they had an idea of making those theories practical and living: the word was "solidarity."

The most brilliant among the writers of this zealous generation was certainly M. Anatole France (Thibaut by his real name), whose eightieth birthday and subsequent funeral have recently been celebrated by the constituted authorities, public corporations, and a good part of the country. In him is to be admired the most fortunate of our writers. The halo of luck which surrounds him is so thick that it seems to conceal his life. There is almost nothing to be said about it: the son of a Parisian bookseller of Angevin origin, M. France had a good classical education, preached Republic under the Empire, and wrote Parnassian verse. He devoted himself then to literary pastiches and trickery — a practice which he never completely abandoned. He published a few books on literary history, and then in 1881 his first great novel, "le Crime de Sylvestre Bonnard", which attracted attention. His critical articles ("la Vie Littéraire") were also successful, but world renown did not come until the "Jérôme Coignard" ("la Rôtisserie de la Reine Pédauque", 1893; "les Opinions de M. Jérôme Coignard", 1893) and his "Bergeret" ("Orme du Mail", 1897; "Mannequin d'Osier," 1897; "Anneau d'Améthyste", 1899; "M. Bergeret à Paris", 1901).

Since then his works have always excited lively interest and discussions, which, if sharp, have been none the less fruitful. Besides, M. France, by a strange and unusual destiny, seems to have had the privilege of passing close to people and problems without understanding them, without respecting them, and also without their daring to object. He attacked the Symbolists cruelly, and was invited by them to share their triumph of 1891, which he accepted with good grace; he denounced Zola for his filth, then threw flowers on his tomb and was carried in triumph by the remnants of Naturalism. He launched against Catholicism and the Ancien Régime harsh, systematic and persistent attacks, and the leaders of the Conservative party looked upon him as a defender of the past. He ridiculed the Academy, despising it to the extent of refusing to become a member; nevertheless he was the candidate of the dukes in 1897, and is still considered in academic circles as the champion of traditional French. Even the republican régime, bourgeois and radical, was not spared — M. France ridiculed it with wit and success, both in France and in foreign countries (he was offered an editorship on the anti-French review the *Nation* of New York, and accepted), which has not prevented his receiving the homages of that régime, or being its patriarch.

Such uninterrupted good fortune is in itself

genius, but it is also claimed that M. France is one of the great writers of our country. His style passes for perfect, harmonious, measured, figured, witty, classic; his thought is considered as sharp as it is profound and balanced.

This opinion, accepted by a large number of people, and many of importance, deserves some consideration. Certainly M. France possesses a Renanian intelligence, enamored of exactitude, physical perception, and science. But his mind hardly gives the impression of flexibility. The "Vie Littéraire" especially is full of his *lacunæ:* he missed Rimbaud, ridiculed Mallarmé, exalted Coppée, Prudhomme and F. Plessys as "real poets." He went through Symbolism and Naturalism without seeing anything. He never showed an interest in the literary effort of those who were seeking and inventing; he never took the trouble to understand them. The new generation owe him nothing but a few sarcasms. The occasional discussions in the series of the "Bergeret" or the "Coignard" have a curious perfume of pedagogy and ignorance. M.

France always explains very clearly that he does not understand; nothing that he fails to perceive or understand exists for him; thus is his world very simple, very small, without a shadow, and devoid of novelty.

After all, he has said it himself: ideas mean little to him; he believes in sentiments. And yet those impulses to which he surrenders are very rudimentary in character; he was able to assimilate neither the refined æsthetic sentiment, nor mysticism, nor philosophic pleasure. He loves solidarity without defining it, progress without discerning it, and the happiness of mankind without believing it. Especially does he love to think like everybody else. He ridiculed those whom the public was ridiculing; he became a radical-socialist with the régime (1896–1910); he praised the War with us all, and, like everybody, became disgusted with it. In his old age he was the kind of a Bolshevik we would all like to be: rich, respected by the bourgeois, whose luxury and prejudices he shared, and whose homage he received, admired by the radicals, who excused his good fortune and opulence in the hope some day to make use of them. Finally the general public loved him, less for his theories and homilies than for his descriptions. Every one of us, at some time or other in our lives, M. France has taken by the body. He possesses the nicely whetted, delicate, greedy senses of the Angevin. He has always treated them well, and in return it is to them that he owes his success. His voluptuous descriptions, his plump and savory images, his musical pages, bear witness to one original quality: "The noon sun darted forth its white and subtle rays. Not a cloud in the sky, nor a breath in the air. Over the vast repose of all things the light alone was dancing, and on the horizon conducted its fiery evolutions. In the deserted mall, the shadows fell heavy and still at the feet of the elms. A road-hand lay asleep in a ditch which borders the ramparts. The birds were still."

M. France expresses this voluptuousness of things and of the body in a scholar's language, polished, archaic, monotonous, often pedantic (in his dialogues, where the characters speak in the same tone, and take great pains to em-

bark on learned digressions), but at the same
time agreeable, for it flows easily, and imposing, for it is always instructive. This attitude, which belongs to his intelligence as well
as to his prose, has procured him a vast
popular success. This licentious and fluent
pedagogue, who always refrained from original
thought, who never penetrated far into the
realm of the intelligence or that of the sentiments, who never doubted himself nor sus-
pected the narrowness of his perceptions, was
bound to impress the crowds. The crowd, as
is well known, would rather fear than respect.
And M. France, by the baseness of his imagination, the frankness of his ignorance, the
elegance of his emptiness, has placed himself
close to us all. He has flattered our flesh
and our human respect. His success is due
especially to what he has not said, not done,
not desired.

It was just that a writer should have a
social triumph, in whom such rare adroitness
was coupled to such a convenient personality,
and it is gratifying to see M. France applauded
by everybody. It is also fortunate that M.

France has no serious influence in French literature. He has contributed nothing either great or new, except perhaps the example of unusual luck and a well managed career. The admirers who surrounded him at la Béchellerie and now cultivate his glory are mostly of the political and official variety. He has been used against neologism, Romanticism, the parliamentary régime; his true "disciples" would be reactionaries, but that doesn't seem to be known, and the crowd admires him as the writer who, like our republican government, has been able to insert democratic sentiments into the framework of the Ancien Régime and the Empire. He has thus become an institution, like the *baccalauréat* and the kilogram.

M. France's life and his apotheosis prove that despite all calumnies the masses are not ungrateful, and know how to reward those who think for them, with them, like them, and are careful not to go beyond them.

BOOKS

Who hasn't read a dozen of "France"? The most typical for me are: "la Vie Littéraire," "l'Orme du Mail" and "les Dieux ont soif." See also M. Gsell's book: "les Matinées de la Villa Saïd" (so useful for the understanding of France), and for the balance, that of M. Brousson: "Anatole France en pantoufles."

CHAPTER X

PAUL BOURGET

And High Bourgeois Literature

WHILE M. France was becoming the official writer of the régime, M. Bourget was accepted as the novelist of the upper middle class. Since then, he has been faithful to them, and they to him. They were made for one another. This class, at first overwhelmed by their political defeats, found subsequently a source of energy and prestige in the very attacks directed against them by their rivals. As the heirs of the moral and intellectual traditions of the Monarchy and the Empire, possessing very important financial resources, holding in the liberal professions, finance, agriculture, and industry a coherent and well-administered estate, they have profited by the discredit of parliaments and ministries. They are an active, hard-working class, in general sound, and curious of intelligence. They proved their great qualities in the War. Firmly established on the *Revue des Deux Mondes*, the *Gaulois*, *l'Echo de Paris*, and the *Journal des Débats*, they occupy a solid position in the world of thought. They like to be *au courant*, they read the books with care, and even buy them. Whatever they may think, they are neither very sensitive, nor very sentimental, nor very complicated, but they are still the best public in France, for they study literature with conviction, attribute great importance to the written word, and will pay for what they like.

During the Dreyfus affair this class went through a severe crisis; they seemed on the point of splitting into two groups: some of their journals were leading them toward the left (*Figaro*), others, the majority, to the right. If they did not regain a clear perception of themselves they were lost. And this is the inestimable service which Bourget did them.

M. Bourget was intelligent, kind-hearted, and already known. Son of a distinguished university official, he had received his education in Auvergne and at Paris. He had experienced the influence of Renan and Taine, and then the reaction to the War of 1870, for him a profound emotional crisis. He had sought his way passionately, and with anxiety. The faith of his childhood had been lost in his gropings. He didn't know where to go: in turn a student of letters, student of medicine, teacher, he wanted to write, and devoted himself to poetry, but without neglecting the novel and criticism. He visited the new School cénacles, where he met Laforgue, to whom he was to be of so great service. His three volumes of poetry ("Vie inquiète", 1875; "Edel", 1878; "les Aveux", 1882) revealed neither original inspiration, nor a powerful sensibility, nor the gift of expression, but finesse, timidity, and a love of suffering. His sensibility was thin, and at the same time extremely eager. He knew his limits, and this knowledge was a source of pain. With his invariable honesty he perceived his mediocrity, and was tortured by it. Having reached thirty and done nothing that satisfied him or matched his desires, he felt the need of discharging his responsibility in the presence of himself and of the world; he took up his masters one by one and demonstrated their errors. Out of this desire for justification, this despair, Paul Bourget's best works were born, the "Essais de Psychologie contemporaine (1881–1883). Here Bourget shows himself so penetrating, so sincere and loyal, that the books have grandeur and beauty. His studies of Taine, Renan, Stendhal, Baudelaire, etc., deserve to be read. While still an indistinct personality, Bourget had subjected himself unresisting to all these teachers, and he gives of them a clear and well-defined image. Taine had fascinated him because of his earnestness and self-assurance; from him Bourget had received that cult of scientific certitude which he would never abandon. Of Naturalism, he had adopted that violent and unfortunate taste for the real, which he held the supreme end of art. But he was sufficiently discerning to see in the Symbolists not only their success, which was actual, but also their primitive and unformed aspiration, the voluptuousness of the subconscious, the pleasure of abandon to that joy which neither our bodies nor our minds can measure, and which nevertheless dominates us. Bourget thus presented a chart of his generation with true lines and colors bright enough to strike the eye. His book attracted attention. In the bourgeois circles where there was a desire for information, where a guide was needed through the modern world and modern literature, he was welcomed, for he was well informed, conscientious, and modest.

His success revealed his vocation. The "Essais de Psychologie" had been a series of portraits composed with obligations to psychological analysis. He set about writing novels, which were themselves a sort of psychological museum of the modern world. He thus remained faithful to the ideas of M. Taine and the scientific method. To be sure he added a great deal, as is evident in "le Disciple" (1889) where pure science was denounced in the person of a young philosopher brought to destruction by a vain love for scientific experimentation. Gradually M. Bourget was led back to the Catholic faith, to monarchical

96

convictions, and traditionalist doctrines. The stages in his "conversion" are marked by his novels: "Idylle tragique" (1891), "la Duchesse Bleue" (1898), "l'Etape" (1901). By this date M. Bourget had reached port, he had ceased to debate with himself and now spoke in public only to teach. This he did in absolute good faith and with a great deal of talent. Each one of his novels is the exposition of a doctrine valuable from the social and moral point of view. From then on he denied himself both art for art and science for science; the Dreyfus affair created in him, as in his contemporaries, a strong desire for action and apostleship. Nevertheless he kept the scientific method as a means of proof, and remained extremely preoccupied with the subconscious, everything that is sensation or perception. This breadth of view, added to his precision of mind and good intentions, has made him, since 1900, the guide of the traditionalist bourgeoisie, and at the same time the master of the psychological novel. The discovery of the formula of the psychological novel *à thèse* was his triumph. Since then he has possessed an immovable public, who ask no more than that he publish regularly a book a year. M. Bourget's literature is a career.

His stories and novels are in general well constructed, and in a manner calculated to hold the attention; they evoke present problems, and impress by an air of veracity. M. Bourget employs an ample and complex intrigue to demonstrate the development of characters and delicate situations. Architecturally, then, the work is good. It delights minds who find amusement and instruction in "true stories", but to the generations who demand that literature be creative and lead them out of reality, his work seems "meager." M. Bourget's style is deplorable: his sentences composed of discordant, formless, and ill-fitting elements, his heteroclite and unlovely vocabulary (he uses shamelessly such words as *facticités*, *implacabilité*, *préraphaélitisme*, *bohémianisme*, etc.), his banal and conscientious images, are really distressing, for he is so evidently honest that it would be a pleasure to like him. His descriptions are colorless and hardly convincing: "I have always felt the beauty of the arts as a man of letters, in other words, a man whose first requirement of a picture or a statue is that it be an excuse for thought"; so he says himself, and on reading him it is quite evident that beyond a few simple and almost brutal sensations, all the rest is imagined. It is "literature", *du chromo*.

Nevertheless having thus rendered a severe judgment on M. Bourget's work, one is bound to state that it attracts sympathy and holds the attention. One feels that he is much more intelligent than everything he has done, better than his books, more loyal and greater than his characters. His considerable influence is due especially to this halo about his head. A whole group of authors write like him and exploit the same vein with almost the same attitudes. A Bazin or a Bordeaux might be cited, and many others less illustrious, who compose for the use of the upper middle class psychological and moral tableaux according to the pseudo-scientific method. All of these novelists possess earnestness and the gift for inventing situations as wearying as those of daily existence, but they miss the rest.

We should be neither proud nor ashamed of these honorable contemporaries. They satisfy a clientèle worthy of esteem, and they answer a need. They are sincere and humble, for they know as well as we the destiny which awaits them. That saddens them, but the sentiment of duty accomplished and a successful career are compensation for the bitterness of the future. They do not cheat: no one is obliged to read them, but their special public does it, and with real pleasure   They cultivate the taste for letters and intellectual curiosity in vast and powerful social classes. And they are so useful to the "younger generation"!

BOOKS

P. Bourget: "Le Disciple", "Essais de Psychologie contemporaine", "L'Etape", "Le Démon de Midi."

V. Giraud: "Les Maîtres de l'heure."

CHAPTER XI

MAURICE BARRES

Literature Raises the Tone

TOWARD 1895 literature was reconciled to service: with Zola it had put itself at the orders of the people, industry, and useful science; Taine had trained it to pedagogy and scientific methods; for Renan even, style was hardly more than a seasoning for erudition; in vain had the Symbolists sought to liberate and exalt poetry, proposing no other goal than its own glory; defeat for the time being had discredited their ideas, and in 1895 French prose, devoid of solid intellectual armor, brilliant passions, or delicate nuance, spoke on an extraordinarily low tone: an emphatic, confused, middle-class vocabulary, constructions feeble and flat, or badly imitated, gave evidence of the misery of a literature obsessed by social preoccupations, and aiming to be "conscientious."

Maurice Barrès' voice, rising suddenly, surprises and delights. This dark, tall youth, with his air of a "Proconsul woeful of life", as Moréas said in the language of the time, had attracted a certain amount of attention about 1883. The son of middle-class Lorraine parents, he was just out of the lycée at Nancy, where he had acquitted himself honorably and come under fruitful influences. From his first years, Barrès (1863–1923) had given evidence of an eminently receptive and curious intelligence. The *internat* had been torture for him, and very young he had learned the odious in human contacts; but this suffering, far from disheartening him, had aroused immense ambitions and an indistinct avidity. Romanticism, which was fading for so many others, was still in him a vital force: he had understood Hugo's "lesson in words" and never forgot the intoxication of that sonorous and sentimental philter; for him Romanticism was not a completed stage, an accumulation of stupidities piled into a corner: he found it a lesson and a delight, and he preserved its best elements. This tendency was reinforced by the influence of Germanic philosophy, which was always to confuse him a little, but gave him nevertheless a few good formulas. He kept intact, however, that intellectual consciousness, that critical faculty, and measured taste, which made him such a complete mind and so entirely congruous to the traditions of our country.

In Barrès the young man, what a marvelous competition of desires! He wants to feel, to act, to understand, to talk especially, for the last is all the rest, plus intoxication. His discouraged parents had given up making him a notary; Barrès was seen in the Latin Quarter and Montmartre, he contributed to the young reviews, he published one which nobody read, he frequented the Decadents and shocked them by the sincerity of his disgust. He carried in him a terrible inaptitude for life, and this contrast with his passion appeared in his body, mind, and destiny; he was one of the first to denounce Taine and Renan and Science, and to comprehend Symbolism, but he was never able to practice it completely or really belong to the group;

he was a poet, and never succeeded in writing verse; mystic and religious, he smiled at the Catholic Church and never became a member; a patriot enamored of authority and command, he would accept neither the Monarchy nor the Demagogy, which last would at least have loaned him power, and he gave his passionate enthusiasm to the poor man whom even misfortune could not make tragic, Boulanger!

Barrès carried his defeat within him and his grandeur is that he knew it, realized it completely. Into such knowledge, no other in the century, except perhaps Chateaubriand, put such constancy and such majesty. Barrès' disaster, renunciation, and apotheosis date from the period following Symbolism and Boulangism (1893–1900). He already had a whole life behind him: now as the author of much admired articles and a series of handsome novels (the "Culte du Moi," which contains the "Jardin de Bérénice", 1891), defender of the new School, Boulangist deputy from Nancy, Barrès adopted action to hide his laziness, mask his awkwardness, and litera-

ture to beguile his passions. Twenty-five
years of politics, honest, monotonous, narrow,
relentless, let him forget that the vast world
would have amused him; twenty volumes of
literature permitted him to nurse and lull
that universal sensuality which nothing could
satisfy ("Roman de l'énergie nationale", 1897–
1903, which contains his finest book: "Leurs
Figures"; "Amori et Dolori Sacrum", 1903;
"Voyage de Sparte", 1905; "la Colline inspirée", 1914; "Jardin sur l'Oronte", 1923). He
thus led a noble life, prisoner by his own
choice, and this man, one of the most direct
intelligences, in sensibility one of the richest
of his age, found in this voluntary poverty
the only compensation worth the name, that
of pride; gestures and speech would take the
place of people, words were the consolation
for things.

The words he left behind are sorcery. He
did not possess, true, the dominating intellect
which discovers behind the fluidity of appearances the solid framework of the real,
constructing for future centuries the cage in
which men will live; the theories he invented

in order to comprehend himself and his age are hardly coherent, nor convincing, and often incomplete: that "cult of the *moi*," which helped him define his pride, is an emblem, rather than a doctrine, and the same for *enracinement* and "eternal Boulangism", which conceal nevertheless instincts profound, direct, resisting. Here, in fact, is the great value of Barrès: his passion is not simple melting and passive voluptuousness, as it seems at first: behind the soft ornaments, Barrès in his clumsy body is a powerful and brutal soul. If his intelligence did not model a world, it could at least impregnate his whole being with firmness, lucidity clear desire. Describing the corrupted parliament, the Baron de Reinach panting with fear at the opening of the Panama affair he says:

"At the end of that day, when the fat Baron found all the loopholes blocked, the circle closes in until he feels the two hands of the strangler around his neck. His accomplices, who had thought at first to escape the peril with him, now work to wall him up. For some time a nuisance, he has now become worse than a suspect. He can thus be considered a corpse in the process of formation. *Jam foetet.* They stamp in their haste to entomb him."

After the death of the financier he concludes: "The Baron Jacques de Reinach makes you think of one of those big rats that gulp the bait and go off to die behind a partition, whence the irritated body poisons the poisoners. The house has to be half torn down. It was to this that the French suddenly set themselves."

Barrès at such moments shows the cruel energy of his nature: vanquished, he admits no vanquisher but himself, and the disaster of the universal disgrace will not overwhelm him so long as he can protest, that is to say, see himself and show himself different from the others. Barrès pushed very far this desire to feel different and alone, born doubtless of natural pride and awkwardness, encouraged by his early failures and difficult successes, hardened by the cult of the *patrie*, from which he took above all a discipline of resistance (against democracy, against internationalism, which he looked upon as great forces for leveling and unification).

Almost alone in his generation Barrès knew the value of sounds, the color of words, the cadence of phrases; he created images capable of moving the senses and astonishing the mind; saying nothing he constantly invented new pleasures and new pains. More than any other man of his age Barrès had the gift of seeing in language a reservoir of forces and of knowing how to use it. If his sonorous sentences are sometimes hollow, one may say that they are so after the fashion of crowns, and deck a royal void. They show that their master lacked neither desire nor strength, but only that cleverness or littleness necessary to cross the low and narrow doors of the treasures of this world.

Freeing literature from servitude, humble and material cares, Barrès restored the prestige formerly given it in France by the great Classics, with their intellectual nobility, by the Romantics, with their apostolic ambition. He did more: his renunciation, not entirely devoid of egoism or of grandeur, continued the Symbolist crusade against the external world. Barrès divined the most intimate suffering of his time and its most essential need: like the Symbolists he turned toward an art of creation, of liberation, where the mind would dominate the flesh, where the artist would be a magician, not copying the prestidigitations of science, but on the contrary strong enough to escape that obsession of cleverness, industry, progress, which weighs upon us like a nightmare, and deceives us.

Barrès, thus struggling, attracted the attention of the newcomers. More than any other he interested the generations which grew up between 1898 and 1912; his eloquence, his lyricism, his intelligence, his passion, especially the majesty of his bearing, and his creative effort, aroused hatred and love. How many young men, like him, have sought to harden their bodies, their souls, their pride! Already the echo of his name extends through the years like these words, in which he summons up the wingèd horse ready to take flight towards solitude and immortality:

"It was in the depths of the ages, and as now the sun was setting. There were great, calm spaces in the heaven above the sea, and the rock cast a shadow on the spring. There stood the horse and the hero. Little precious group on the immense scene."

BOOKS

Barrès: "Huit jours chez M. Renan", "le Culte du Moi", "Leurs Figures", "le Voyage de Sparte", "la Colline inspirée", and all the rest, if possible.

R. Gillouin: "M. Barrès."

CHAPTER XII

French Prose from 1900 to 1914

[MME. LOIE FULLER TO THE RUSSIAN BALLET]

IN the evolution of French prose there are no sharp breaks: change is constant, but also slow. After 1900 people were tired of Naturalism; Science as a cult had failed to satisfy; Symbolism was numb with fatigue; nevertheless a Naturalist tradition continued, and young men like the admirable C.-L. Philippe (1874–1909), strongly influenced by the Russians, remained faithful. The scientific spirit still reigned in history, which aspired to no more than the mass of documents or the reconstruction of the past (Lavisse, Aulard), and in literary history and criticism, which aimed at mathematical exactitude (M. Lanson), but the first fervor of the religion of science was gone, and the public was losing interest.

From 1900 to 1914 France rested in material prosperity. People talked of war as of a fashionable scandal or the ruin of Sodom, but they were acquiring, amassing, and enjoying life. The crops were good, factories multiplied, in the cities workmen as well as the middle class attended the theater, went to Luna Park, and admired the first cinemas. Security, luxury, social laws, the progress of industry, which introduced the automobile into our habits — all conspired to make life calm and agreeable. People felt the need of distractions. They sought them, and successive governments, with an eye to reëlection, strove to furnish | the masses with comforts and pleasures. Frenchmen, always impressionable, abandoned themselves to felicity and desired to diversify its course. The "*vains vifs*", said Stendhal, speaking of us, his compatriots; quick to comprehend, to feel, to love, avid of new sensations — thus he painted us, and without believing that he had spoken praise.

Romanticism had developed this characteristic by exalting sensibility at the expense of the intelligence. Like Rousseau, Chateau-

briand had been a "sensation teacher." The
pleasure of acting, reasoning, judging, had
receded to the background, supplanted by
the voluptuousness of perception and passionate enthusiasm. Thus through the whole
course of the nineteenth century French sensibility had been enriched; then the Goncourts,
giving it a language of its own, had refined it,
their Academy maintained their influence,
and Symbolism, though opposed to Hugo's
verbalism, tended to continue the work of the
great Romantics by teaching that greater and
greater importance should be attached to
sensation and sentiment, that they should be
cultivated and considered something divine.

Verlaine had made religious mysticism again
fashionable, Mallarmé revealed the pure æsthetic sentiment; all of them adored music
and helped establish the reign of 'Wagner.
The Bayreuth pilgrimages became crusades;
Debussy, more subtle, was not less intoxicat-
ing. Even painting, fascinated by the success
of music, drifted toward impressionism, of
which Monet furnished il ustrious examples.
Literature soon followed. Julien Viaud (Loti,

1850–1922) was for thirty years one of the most popular French writers. An officer in the navy, he was content to describe in a flowing style, amorphous, moving, glittering, the spectacles which filed before his eyes or the mirages flickering in his imagination. His vague ideas, indistinct religiosity, languorous melancholy, his formless and tricky style, hardly deserve immortal reputation, but he was close to his public and pleased them. Then came a flood of sensation art. The object was to "vibrate" all the parts of the body: Huysmans wrote in images taken from the kitchen, Barrès aimed at color and music, France was libertine and gluttonous; Mme. Colette, admirable novelist, created beasts, and stirred the deepest forces of the animal nature; many tried to tempt the jaded senses with exoticism: Farrère in particular, who succeeded so well (born in 1876), and far above him, Doctor Mardrus, with his marvelous translations of the "Arabian Nights." A few, of cold but adroit temperament, cultivated the sensational, scandal even, and pretended to lend it decency by decking it out in pseudo-

classical style (such as M. A. Hermant) or in
worldly wisdom, as did M. M. Prévost. These
luxuries were usually coarse enough, rudimentary and uncoördinated; few of these authors
were endowed with original or intense sensibility, but their descriptions were piquant or
carefully written, and they held the reader's
attention. The best of them was doubtless
the philosopher Bergson. His fluid, imaginative style, and certain of his theories hostile
to the primacy of the intelligence, indicating
the sensibility as the source of knowledge,
may be considered the highest expression of
these tendencies.

This overflow of pleasures, abandon to the
instinctive forces of the being, chaos of discordant joys, finally brought a reaction in circles faithful to the veneration of science and
intellectual culture. In 1902 appeared a terrible book: "les Amants de Venise", by
Charles Maurras. This book, of lacerating
harshness and clairvoyance, presented a thesis
opposed to the one accepted by all the fashionable novelists; Maurras saw sentiment as the
great enemy of man, and proclaimed the duty

of struggling against it. And this was not a simple fantasy. Maurras grouped around him numerous friends, became the leader of a School. His precise, coherent, inclusive doctrine sought to free French sens bility from its intoxication, to dethrone revolutionary ideas, Romantic spirituality, and the republican régime. He was strong enough to found a daily (*Action française*, 1910) and collect around him several reviews, of which the best known was the *Revue Critique*. His criticism, at times heavy, but always powerful, his disinterestedness, his tenacity, quickly gave him an important position. Romanticism was attacked from all sides ("le Romantisme français", by Pierre Lasserre, 1907, campaign of the *Marges*, campaign of Benda against M. Bergson . . .).

But there is no struggling against a torrent: one can only turn its course. There was lack of a few writers of genius in the *Action française* group, which became more and more absorbed in politics. Meanwhile the whole world was sending France its invitations to feel (translations of Kipling, Dostoievski,

d'Annunzio); Chaliapine played "Boris" at the
Opera, and Serge de Diaghilef brought us the
Russian ballets, beautiful, and at the same
time so strange. With them the Orient penetrated us; no longer the divagations of a Loti,
pale chromos, but the warm accentuated
colors, and brutal, well-rhythmed sound. Its
supple, taut body brushed us; a mystic, metal-
lic soul imposed its frenzy upon us. The *Nouvelle Revue Française*, founded in 1909, would
admit neither the supremacy nor the denial of
Romanticism; they pretended to utilize its
lessons: without renouncing the pleasures of
the senses and the soul, they would select
those pleasures, seek them methodically, regu-
late and exploit them. Fusion of a clear and
subtle intelligence with a sensibility full of all
the modern joys — such was their end. Directed by Gide, Copeau, J. Schlumberger,
Claudel, etc., they aspired to be unaware of
nothing in this world, but still maintain the
supremacy of Mind. They encouraged an
unadorned style which, without destroying
the voluptuous, rendered it more delicate,
less external. As early as 1910 their influence

was considerable; they could soon boast of remarkable works: the "Barnabooth" of Valery Larbaud (1912), catalogue of the pleasures of the millionaire of twentieth century Europe, is of astonishing charm. The emotions, perpetually aroused by the most modern forms of life, are guided and exploited by an acute intelligence, and sifted by a harmonious, softly colored style. Others with more force and less charm, such as the Tharaud, furnished the example of a dense and well-directed descriptive style ("Fête Arabe", 1912), while one voice still rose in final adieu to sentimental Romanticism about to vanish and give way to a more violent, more somber art, and we read the last volumes of the "Jean Christophe" of M. Romain Rolland (ten volumes, from 1904 to 1912)

1914 marks the highest point in this effort to feel: 1914, aviation, the Caillaux trial, the first novel of Proust, a year red like a face confused with pleasure and fear. Thanks to this cultivation of our senses, France found herself a country of refinement unprecedented in the universe; body, mind, and soul —

everything was enriched beyond measure, ripe to enjoy and suffer. Never, at any time in our history, had we possessed a being so complex, resonant, ornate. No more the verbal and exterior sensibility of Romanticism, but exaltation of all the senses, expectation of the whole being, desire imperious and precise, need so violent that it becomes creator. The adolescent of 1914 looks on the world with covetous and caressing eyes. He opens to everything, determined to understand, to enjoy, to act, and dance.

BOOKS

Maurras: "Les Amants de Venise."
Valery Larbaud: "A. O. Barnabooth."
Romain Rolland: the first three "Jean Christophe", which are very beautiful.
Loti: "L'Inde, sans les Anglais."
J. and J. Tharaud: "La Fête Arabe", etc.

CHAPTER XIII

French Poetry from 1900 to 1914,
or Purification

WHILE prose, faithful to its social rôle, was drunk with all the sensations obtainable from the body, material life, the society of men, poetry, carried along by the desire which had dominated it since Rimbaud, seemed to withdraw from the crowd, from things, and from the present. A Romantic current still persisted, but especially in writers of foreign birth like Verhaeren or Mme. de Noailles, who, in a slightly obsolete genre, cut a figure as a great poet. Rostand (1868–1920), to be sure, gave the crowd the illusion that the clinking of words and superficial emotions of the heart and senses might still inspire a modern, but it is now easy to see that "Cyrano" (1898) was a mirage. Of Rostand's work there will remain no more than is left after a performance of legerdemain:

a few tricks, a regret that all that can be false, and the esteem of the good public, which always admires cleverness. ("Chantecler", 1910.)

In 1900 the great verbal Romanticism was as dead as classical intellectualism. It no longer satisfied profound and sincere needs, as in 1820, but only survivals. Furthermore, the language in its transformations had robbed the Alexandrine of its traditional qualities. The final disappearance of the pronunciation of mute syllables, the tendency to accentuate certain syllables in the word, together with changes in vowel quantities under the influence of time and foreign languages, all made it impossible to continue the poetry of the eighteenth and nineteenth centuries except by profound modifications of the old technique. Love of the past might inspire a desire to return to classical formulas, as in the case of J. Gasquet and J.-M. Bernard, but this was a chimera, and these poets, despite their talent, were unable to carry their generation with them, or even to win a place in the first rank. Their verse rings hollow.

Only Symbolism and its inventions (free verse, *vers libéré*, the poem in prose) could give young, eager poets the new instrument they needed. Symbolism was levied on from all sides; there were attempts to fuse it with Naturalism (the Naturist School of Saint-Paul-Roux, the Unanimist School with Jules Romains, a brutal but gifted writer, who aimed to reveal the soul of the crowd, so dear to the Naturalists, by the methods of the Symbolist poet, and who succeeded in bringing together a remarkable group: Vildrac, Chennevière, Durtain). Not less clever in taking advantage of Symbolism and the Symbolist inventions, but less virile in inspiration, were the poets usually called *"fantaisistes"*, among whom P.-J. Toulet (1867–1920) will remain as the clearest-marked type ("Contrerimes"). Finally a great many among the Symbolists were content to qualify and repeat their inventions, so that the public, through familiarity, might come to love them as "reasonable". P. Fort, in his immense production, and H. de Régnier furnished the example and were followed by a crowd of feeble souls. A few courageous ones resisted and maintained the Symbolist discoveries in their integrity. Of these faithful E Dujardin is doubtless the best.

But of all the descendants of Symbolism, the strongest, the most vital, and the best inspired, were the Catholic group. This should not cause wonder, for Symbolism, to endure, demanded a strict moral discipline; if it had a meaning, that meaning lay in a revolt against the material world, and faith in the spiritual domain; if it was to attract attention, it must vanquish this universe and offer the image of another world, beautiful, free, of within. Catholicism afforded priceless resources, and from 1900 to 1914 the three great poets of France were three mystics: Jammes, Claudel, and Péguy. All three attempted an imposing effort to snatch poetry from the world, purify it, and present an image of supernatural perfection. Jammes, a peasant, hardly master of himself, did not go so far as the others in this struggle, but he had charm, a pleasant and spirited imagination, a great gift for the image, tears, and unction. His "Géorgiques chrétiennes", despite pagan accents, have a delightful childish suppleness, a tone of candor which commands respect, a white, brilliant, radiant color. All his poetry unfolds like a procession across the fields, close to the soil, above which it scarcely seems to rise, but raising over it nevertheless a towering mystery.

Claudel (born in 1868) knew better how to tear himself away. His wandering life as consul, a soul barded with theology, afforded him better protection. In his first works there is a certain inaptitude for life, a need of virgin atmosphere, unspoiled words, names which evoke nothing familiar, fresh rhythms, solitude, which all bring him close to certain of the great Symbolists. Moved by Rimbaud, taught by Mallarmé, molded by foreign countries and foreign ways (for he was able to understand the United States and China, one after the other), harrowed by harsh passions, awkward, captive, irritated, Claudel said at first in obscure dramas the aspiration of his soul to order, not the order of the mathematicians, but the order that each man carries mysteriously within him, the seal of God

124

upon his creature and creation. To the end of his own freedom he fashioned a whole universe of anxious faces, calling, groping unwearied ("Tête d'Or", "l'Echange", "la Ville", etc.). Gradually his tone ascended, and in certain of his poems attained a high degree of nobility. In "les Muses", he said:

O mon âme! Le poème n'est point fait de ces lettres que je plante comme des clous, mais du blanc qui reste sur le papier.

O mon âme, il ne faut concerter aucun plan!

O mon âme sauvage, il faut nous tenir libres et prêts,

Comme les immenses bandes fragiles d'hirondelles quand sans voix retentit l'appel automnal!

O mon âme impatiente, pareille à l'aigle sans art! Comment ferions-nous pour ajuster aucun vers? à l'aigle qui ne sait pas faire son nid même?

Que mon vers ne soit rien d'esclave! Mais tel que l'aigle marin qui s'est jeté sur un grand poisson,

Et l'on ne voit rien qu'un éclatant tourbillon d'ailes et l'éclaboussement de l'écume!

Thus does the poetry of Paul Claudel take its flight, in a powerful, sometimes painful effort tearing itself from the soil. Claudel is a French peasant, a bourgeois from Champagne; in him an acute sense of all material realities, the need of living by the body, dwells side by side with insatiable, profound, spontaneous spiritual ambition.

The same needs, the same tendencies, dominate Péguy (1873–1914), but his suffering and his death have given him a halo of grandeur and purity to which none among the living can aspire.

He came out of Dreyfusism, which he had practiced as an apostleship. He 'adored France, and more than France, disinterest. He also loved glory, and would have desired happiness, but for their sake he would never sacrifice his isolation. A peasant, graduate of the Normal School, poor, burdened with a family, badly armed as prose writer, poet, and salesman, Péguy was clear-sighted enough to perceive and proclaim the spiritual thirst of his contemporaries. He wanted to give France a new mysticism. He had founded in 1899 the "Cahiers de la Quinzaine", where he wrote with a group of revolutionary friends (Vuillard, Romain Rolland, etc.). It was there that he fought to the end, and in terrible

moral solitude, the struggle which was to lead
him to the battle of the Marne, where at last
he won, with peace, freedom, silence, the accomplishment of his destiny. Péguy suffered, in fact, he so strong and so noble, at not
knowing the words he needed. In his groping
poetry, and especially in his labored, desperate
prose, there are grandeur, beauty, new effects.
He underlines with charcoal all the contours
of his thought and sentiment, out of honesty,
and also in order that they have nothing in
common with the thoughts and sentiments
sold in the street. Sprung from the crowd, he
drew away from them; his calls to the élite
were deadened by his hoarse and monotonous
voice. The ball which killed him found him
alone on the summit of a knoll.

Nevertheless, Jammes, Claudel, Péguy
guided the poetry of their time. With them it
fled the social, the theater in particular, for
Claudel's drama was entirely of within, and
could hardly be played. This slow drying-up
of the theater in France from 1900 to 1914 was
one of the most curious phenomena of the
time. A few comic writers in prose (Courte-

line, T. Bernard, Caillavet) and a few estimable professionals (Curel) obtained a hearing, but the theater, despite the efforts of the "Vieux Colombier" to rescue it from social servitude, almost ceased to be a literary genre. In 1914 this decline was manifest; on all sides the new generations sought the discovery of an art which would be creative, and not imitation of the forms of external life, pleasure of invention and not of reminiscence. They turned eagerly toward the canvases called "Cubist", exhibited by a group of painters and commented on by a young poet, Guillaume Apollinaire (1880–1918). The latter pointed to his friends, Picasso, Braque, Derain, as the guides who, by tearing painting from its old habits of copying, had given it sovereignty. In fact in these pictures the material world is no more than a means to evoke æsthetic impressions. The Cubists do not represent objects. They suggest sentiments, thanks to lines, colors, schemes taken from the material world, simplified and disciplined. Apollinaire desires to do the same in poetry; he tries and succeeds. ("Alcools", 1913.)

Meanwhile Jammes, buried under the mass of his writings, Claudel, prisoner of the high functions entrusted him by the Republic, and Péguy delivered of life, have left the field free and passed on the task; they have cleaned poetry of many prejudices, preoccupations, habits, but this was not enough: a new generation appears and sings with Apollinaire:

> *Fermons nos portes*
> *A double tour,*
> *Chacun apporte*
> *Son seul amour.*

BOOKS

Mme. de Noailles: "Le visage émerveillé."

F. Jammes: "Le roman du lièvre", "Clara d'Ellébeuse", "Géorgiques chrétiennes."

P. Claudel: "L'Echange", "L'Otage", "L'Annonce faite à Marie", "Corona benignitatis", "Connaissance de l'Est."

Péguy: "Le mystère de la charité de Jeanne d'Arc", "Victor Marie comte Hugo."

G. Apollinaire: "Alcools."

CHAPTER XIV

MARCEL PROUST

Inventor of Pleasures

FRENCH poetry was aspiring to free itself from the servitude of the external world to enjoy in peace its art and its soul, prose in an opposed effort was attempting to exhaust all the pleasures of things and of beings, when the War burst forth. Magnificent pleasures had been known before, but this last was so burning, so exclusive, that it destroyed all others at a single stroke. Heroic disciplines for isolation had been discovered, but this last in truth made the others seem play, for it cut the thread of all life. With the War all words lost their significance: humanity, progress, pity — what now did they mean? In the universal upheaval of conditions and sensibilities, all vocables were voided of their content. In the midst of the immense fracas of cannon, cries of enthusiasm and hate, there reigned a strange silence.

Men still wrote, mechanically, but brought forth sounds or acts and not words. An Albert de Mun, a Barrès, a France, a Rolland, could shriek or groan, but they did not speak. Alone, mysterious, there rose above the carnage a few voices still endowed with articulate words. They came as if from a solitude which had protected them. They had not been extinguished with all that was vanishing, for they were not of it. Thus new men appeared, and new reputations: Marcel Proust, whose first great book dates from 1914, Paul Valéry, who published his "Jeune Parque" in 1917, and André Gide, whose work, already known, shone with a bright luster in the light of the War. I shall speak of all three in turn with the pleasure and the uneasiness that one feels in judging what he has lived. I shall mention Proust first, for death has achieved his destiny and allows us to judge him entire, or such as he is concealed behind reticences henceforth eternal.

Marcel Proust, son of rich bourgeois, born

in 1873, had never possessed beauty, despite the gentleness of his eyes. He had a certain repellent flaccidity: white flesh, a varnished elegance, gestures vague and complicated; nevertheless his generosity, his goodness, his extreme niceness, commanded affection. At the end of his life he seemed dim and swollen, combining with indescribable refinement a vexatious negligence of his person. One pitied him and would have liked to give him the tenderness he needed, which he solicited and repulsed by an undue anxiety to please and obtain pleasure from others. One felt him a Jew in body, sick, and hardly normal.

From infancy, his bad health which tormented his parents, his idleness, his wealth, his snobbery, and his Jewish race had been causes of isolation. Not that he was deprived of friends or social contacts, but he had acquired them, more than he possessed them. Besides, despite social success, he remained a prisoner of his illness and of his timidity, which never permitted him freedom or independence. He was able, then, to meet a great number of people, rub against them, but he never trusted them, and lived alone with their images. They were only objects of desire or subjects for speculation. His extreme refinement, his remarkable culture, his over-excited sensibility, made him most exacting, and this very eagerness kept him aloof from other men. It was so violent as to be something monstrous. I remember my fright at seeing Proust drink, eat, talk, and discourse on pleasure. This being, so fragile, so distant, was insatiable, and when a draft would have killed him, dreamed only of entering the furnace in search of a new joy. He lived in a fashionable set, quite narrow after all, where he was pampered, for he had published a precious and subtle book ("les Plaisirs et les Jours", 1896) and some articles on Ruskin, whom he worshiped (*Mercure de France,* 1900). He talked about a great work he was preparing, and his friends were inclined to admire him.

In 1913 he tried to get published "Du côté de chez Swann." The publishers balked at the singularity of the style and subject. He had to have it printed at his own expense.

But the immediate success of the volume gave Proust his vengeance, and opened him the *Nouvelle Revue Française*, which subsequently founded a chapel in his memory, where his cult is practiced with a zeal which is occasionally indiscreet (special number, January 1, 1923).

The War was a torture for Proust, but did not interrupt his work. Sick, shut up in his room, which he now left only at rare intervals, and then usually after midnight to see a few close friends, Proust continued in himself the work on which he had been long engaged. He had come out of the period of "time lost", when he had lived for the sake of seeing people, accumulating impressions, for agitation. He had entered the creative phase: time regained; the War, its strangeness, at last placing him in a solitude entirely apart from men, giving him that silence necessary to bestow upon sentiments and desires their full resonance. He who had never been satisfied by any simple impression come from without, sought now to create for himself and others new combinations of pleasure and joy. Isolating and read-

justing the elements he carried within him
(memories of joys and pains), he made a new
world, turned not toward the act nor toward
the idea, but to the voluptuous alone.

Thus he wrote "A la recherche du temps
perdu", a sort of narrative in the form of
memoirs, depicting the life of a whole group
as it is reflected in a single sensibility: "Le
côté de Guermantes", (1920–1921), " A l'om-
bre des Jeunes filles en fleurs" (1918), "So-
dome et Gomorrhe" (1921–1922), "la Prison-
nière" (1923). This novel is a pleasure, or
rather a world of pleasures, for such was certainly the intention of Proust in composing
it. His end was not to write history, or he
would have presented the events, and not
simply their reflection. These volumes are
of astonishing reality from the point of view
of human observation, creation of states of
being, and at the same time astonishing fiction from the point of view of the narrative,
circumstances, the social picture. Proust
mingles an intense poetry (for he transports
us into events and sentiments fantastic,
unusual, complex) with an occasionally re-

pellent prosaism, which comes from his taste for material things. The same contrasts in his style, which is without form or reserve, but supple, sinuous, nicely calculated to flatter, and constructed, it seems, in view of a perpetual crescendo offering, for Proust liked to give his reader constantly something to feel. He thus piled up images, descriptions, digressions, sensations, theories, with the profusion of a cabinet-maker of the Second Empire. The result, incongruous, lacked neither pleasantness nor grace. For example Proust's hero, who contemplates his mistress sleeping beside him:

"Continuing to hear, to gather up from moment to moment the murmur of her pure breath, soothing as an imperceptible breeze, it was a whole physiological existence which was there before me; as long as I lay on the sand in the moonlight, I remained there watching her, listening to her. Sometimes it seemed that the sea was rising, that the tempest could be felt even in the bay, and I placed myself against her to listen to the rumbling snore of her breath."

These lines show how extraordinary is

Proust's art of separating (not analyzing, as is usually said, quite wrongly), of combining and of bringing out the resonance of each impression. Proust's talent consists in his ability to isolate impressions which had previously passed unnoticed or disregarded, to bring them together with other impressions quite different, as opposed as possible, and to discover perceptible relations between them (his portrait of the man-woman, Charlus; of the artist-beast, Morel; of love-disgust, the hero and Albertine; of virtue-ignominy, Mlle. Vinteuil, etc.). He thus creates a true world, for each part is perceptible and the whole bound together by solid connections of opposition or analogy; and entirely new, for it is delivered of the real, of imitation of society, free of the laws of the material and moral world. Nothing had been seen before which resembled the universe of Proust.

Besides, he did not pursue beauty, which meant comparatively little to him, and of which he entertained a rather formalistic conception: his book, though admirably combined, well constructed, has nothing supreme, either in point of view of frankness or of daring. Proust is neither a moralist (for the absolute, the perfection of God, touch him less than the intensity of the physical impression) nor a courageous immoralist, for he cares little if people despise, ridicule, or sully the things that have given him the most intense and original pleasures. Prisoner of his own voluptuousness, he does not perceive its intellectual outline, and is ignorant of the form it takes in others.

Such are the limits of his genius. Proust came into our literature to create a garden of Armida, astonishing, solitary, where grow only flowers of unknown scents. He really invented new pleasures, new forms of physiological and psychic life, giving thus an answer in the very midst of the War to the hopes of the generation that was dying. But his success made him drunk. He was unable to dominate it, judge it, organize it, to make it a work of art or an object of perfect knowledge. He remains attached to it, as it to him, and they cannot be separated. In it he has left ugliness, and engraved genius.

Marcel Proust

BOOKS

"Du côté de chez Swann", at least. And if possible the whole work (sickness, sea voyage, summer-resort, château life). On Proust, I know of no important study which satisfies me entirely. Nevertheless, Léon Pierre-Quint's book, "Marcel Proust", is very interesting, and the essay of the Duchess de Clermont-Tonnerre, "Proust et Montesquiou", extremely amusing.

CHAPTER XV

PAUL VALERY

or The Voice of Silence

THE War, which destroyed cathedrals and millions of young men, also completed the destruction of classic poetry, Romantic lyrism, and the traditional forms of versification. Between what was felt and suffered, and those measured forms of expression, the disproportion was too great. These new impressions, connected with nothing in the past, had in them something terrifying. The old people saw the War as a sort of nightmare, an atrocious crisis to be borne patiently without understanding. They knew very well that if they survived, the old ways of life could be again resumed. The adolescents, on the contrary, for whom this shock was the first experience of life, accepted it as natural. The War was a school; they let it model their habits, sensibility, and intelligence. Insta-

bility, danger, haste, became familiar to them;
they learned to find them pleasant, and rejected as tedious the slow disciplines of the
past, expression of a time when everything
was certain, well-established, built to last. In
the youngest, then, the most sensitive and the
most perspicacious, there was formed a current of indescribable violence. They demanded pleasures piercing, short, intense as
spasms, which would take them out of reality,
and give them something fresh, something
new and hard. Not to understand was of
little importance to men who had grown up in
the midst of the cruel, mad incoherence of a
War: what they wanted was to escape from the
nightmare of the real. Between them and
their elders, for whom the catastrophe was
only a brutalizing incident, doubtless transi-
tory, and who kept their ideal of peace, was
immediately established a misunderstanding
which nothing could remove, for it was sprung
from an essential opposition of desires. It
was, in truth, only the consummation of the
crisis opened by Symbolism, but violently pre-
cipitated by the War. For forty years men

had fumbled toward a separation of poetry from the social and material world. Now the events themselves accomplished the rupture and gave it gigantic extension. But some among the writers and artists were not surprised, for they had felt the storm coming. When, in 1917, Satie, Picasso, and Cocteau found themselves ready to give "Parade", a bitter and inspired parody of the vain seductions of the modern world, final liquidation of the Russian ballets and exoticism, they had been long carrying it within them. Satie emerged out of twenty years of obscurity and labor. He blossomed suddenly like the little reviews (*Nord-Sud*, for example) and those poets, unknown yesterday, to-day passionately admired by the young generation, who saw in Jacob, in Reverdy, their true masters.

These poets, the leaders of the Cubist group with Apollinaire, methodically organized a literary art based upon the independence of the mind in relation to all other objects. They furnished striking examples ("Ardoises du Toit", by Reverdy; "Cornet à dés", by Jacob), which the crowd found ridiculous and also disturbing. But suddenly, out of the silence, there rose a voice which immediately justified the innovators. The "general public" almost understood, and Valéry was recognized as one of France's most perfect poets.

He was forty-five (1917). He had made his beginnings in poetry twenty-five years before. Then he had just come from Montpellier, and was established in Paris, where he frequented Mallarmé, his initiator, and read eagerly the books of Poe who, with Vinci, was among those who contributed most to the formation of his intelligence. He wrote poems, denying that he was a poet, and without ascribing to them more importance than to any other pleasant or salutary exercise. Valéry held aloof, not from friendships, but from ambition, and a member of a group who were in the act of winning glory and giving themselves to the public, he dodged both the success and the notoriety. He was considered bizarre, but no one took offense, for he attracted irresistibly. Then the years passed, Valéry was talked of no more; it was said that he was working in mathematics and earning his living as secretary to a powerful business man. Some might have thought that he had renounced, or that he was biding his time. Either formula would have been false as a description of the solitary and fruitful task which the poet was performing.

Valéry has not said what he did during those long years of contemplation, but we can divine the course of his thoughts and his work from the way in which he judged life and men. The man who declared to Gide: "Sentimentality and pornography are twin sisters, I detest them . . ." had not retired out of laziness, or to enjoy peace. He had high ambitions, aiming not at glory, and not at obscurity, which is a sort of inverted pride, as vain as it is shameful. He advanced toward a precise goal. Literature meant little to him: it bored him, and faithful here to the ideas of Mallarmé, he knew all the imperfection and deception contained in the completed work of art. On the contrary, he had a high ideal of power, and a passion for intelligence, not simply the intelligence which measures and calculates, but that which constructs and creates, which is the very reason of the universe, whose paths it traces, sometimes even unconsciously. His admiration was the man who conceives and understands how things are done, how acts are thought, and men live. "I have always acted," he said, "to the end of making myself a potential individual," and in his extraordinary "Soirée avec M. Teste", he gave a precise definition of his aspirations:

"Every great man is marred by an error . . . genius is easy, fortune is easy, divinity is easy. I should like simply to say how the thing is conceived."

Such was M. Teste, absolute master of all concepts, and capable of interpreting and analyzing the mechanism, the methods of existence and action which each man uses in being. Such M. Valéry wanted to be, sure thus of becoming the true poet (ποιητής, one who makes). With the methods of Mallarmé, he adopted the ambition of Rimbaud. And convinced that nothing is worth while except that rare inner power of conception and creation, persuaded that "activity" resides in the mind alone, he dared say:

"The incoherence of a discourse depends on

the listener. The mind seems to me to be so made that it cannot be incoherent to itself."

The only object of effort, then, is the completion of the mind. As for the rest, the mind, once made, will produce according to its own rhythm; if the work has been well done, there will be nothing to criticize. If this inner work has been badly done, it is useless to pretend to any sort of perfection in external production. When in 1917 Valéry took the floor, there was heard simply the voice of silence, the direct expression of his mind, with no other object than faithfully to follow the movement of that mind, which had been fashioned by so many efforts.

> *Et qui donc peut aimer autre chose*
> *Que soi-même? . . .*
> (*Fragments du* "Narcisse.")

Thus entirely imbued with an order, an intelligence which he questions no longer and which he need no longer even will, Valéry produces, a pure poet, free from all servitude save that which results from the full possession of himself by his mind:

Paul Valéry

J'ai perdu mon propre mystère;
Une intelligence adultère
Exerce un corps qu'elle a compris.

Now he has only to listen to the words spring within him. Those which his intelligence accepts are stamped with a natural harmony, mysterious perhaps for the heedless, perceptible nevertheless if one can only abandon himself to their charm. And as they have passed through him, they are impregnated with all his qualities. Although his poetry has no other end than to be poetry, it possesses (perhaps unknown to the poet), sensibility, resonance, voluptuousness, passion, for Valéry's solitude has purified everything and destroyed nothing. It has robbed the passions and desires of their base attachments, but preserves them nevertheless as pastime.

Nous marchons dans le temps
Et nos corps éclatants
Ont des pas ineffables
Qui marquent dans les fables.

Through patience which is strength, isolation which is genius, Valéry has understood everything: an order new and enchanting, words evocative and beautiful, thoughts profound as they are firm, sensibility steeped in light.

He has achieved what never before had been seen in any literature: the voice and the intelligence of man rising serene, alone above the world, which they comprehend, and repudiate.

BOOKS

P. Valéry: "Charmes"; "Eupalinos"; "Une soirée avec M. Teste."
A. Thibaudet: "P. Valéry."

CHAPTER XVI

ANDRE GIDE

or The Triumph of Desire

WE have seen contemporary French literature swept along by two opposed tendencies: the need, the greedy search for sensation, which seems to dominate our prose in the last half century, and on the other hand the effort toward isolation, abstraction, the creation of a spiritual world, which seems to be the goal and dream of our modern poetry. One may say that all of our writers have been subject to one of these tendencies. Some have been influenced by first one and then the other; very few minds have been powerful, supple enough to be possessed by both instincts at the same time, and to desire to nurse them both together. But André Gide is of these last. Thus he has taken the place of a leader among us and his name become a symbol. His works and his enemies have made him the champion of the "new spirit" in French literature.

The passions which swirl around him, the depth of his thought, the complexity of his sensibility, and the respect I feel for him, make difficult the task of definition which I have undertaken; nevertheless I cannot evade, for Gide is linked to everything that interests us.

It would be easy to discover in the life itself of André Gide the struggle and competition between the two forces: sensualism, spirituality. Descended from a distinguished Protestant family, Gide (born in 1869) has connections with Normandy and the South. At twenty he comes in contact with the Symbolist movement and frequents Mallarmé, whose personality as much as his doctrines impresses him, and engraves in him that faculty of contemplation which will remain one of his most precious resources. His first works, impregnated with Symbolism, already possess that grave, profound tone which belongs to him alone ("Cahiers d'André Walter", 1891 "Poésies d'André Walter",

1892, "Traité du Narcisse", 1892, "la Tentative Amoureuse", 1893, "Voyage d'Urien", 1893).

But from 1895, travel, the emboldening of his mind, his heart, all his being (the meeting with Wilde) make him an original and powerful writer. After a gesture of farewell to Symbolism, Gide concentrates his attention on the great problem which will henceforth absorb him: how to be strong enough to enjoy everything and give one's self to nothing; how to be pure enough, complete enough, to conceive God? ("Paludes", 1895; "Nourritures Terrestres", 1897; "le Prométhée mal enchaîné", 1899; "le Roi Candaule", 1901; "l'Immoraliste", 1902; "Saül", 1902; "Prétextes", 1903; "le Retour de l'Enfant prodigue", 1909; "la Porte étroite", 1909; "Nouveaux Prétextes", 1911; "Isabelle", 1911.) The years give him authority, the *Nouvelle Revue Française*, in whose foundation he participates, spreads his name and reputation. In 1914 he publishes "les Caves du Vatican", one of the most daring of his books. His silence during the War is only a means to work: "la Sym-

phonie Pastorale", 1920, his extraordinary
"Dostoïewski", 1923, the various fragments
and *morceaux choisis* published in 1920–1924,
his strange novel, "les Faux Monnayeurs"
(1926), his bold memoirs, as beautiful as they
are dangerous ("Si le Grain ne meurt" . . .
1927) show the effort of that intelligence and
that sensibility stretched to their utmost in
order to contain and conciliate opposing tendencies.

Each one of his works is an attempt in this
direction and at the same time a temptation
rejected. Gide is possessed by his subjects,
his characters. He delivers himself from them
by producing the work of art One can understand this theory, which he has frequently
enunciated, only by perceiving his marvelous
love for the human being. No one, in our
time, has been able, with equal intensity, to
see, feel, and conceive in terms of man. Some
think in systems, or in syllogisms, or in rhetorical periods. Gide, one may say, thinks in
men, in personalities. Only the living and
complete synthesis which constitutes a man
has value for him. That is why he is such a

great novelist and critic, and at the same time a sort of educator, a "pastor."

There is no tendency in him, if it obsesses him, which does not become man. There is no tendency in him which will let him rest until it has won from him a human form, whether he make of it the hero of a novel or one of his disciples. He thus creates around him a series of worlds, satisfying his endless need of sensation, and freeing himself. He frees himself both by will and necessity, in order to feel again, create again, for once produced, the living creature (hero of a novel or disciple), detaches himself from us and possesses his own destiny.

Gide's books must not, then, be taken for successive confessions, but for exhibitions, dialogues between Gide and the offerings of life. Hence that critical and at the same time creative attitude; hence also that surprising variety in tone, sentiment, inspiration. Gide is the most gifted writer in modern France and the most skillful, the only prose writer who has been able to profit fully from Symbolism without remaining subject to it. The musical quality of his style is in fact constantly given fresh form by the characters to whom he lends it.

Ménalque cries, "O earth excessively old and so young, if you knew the bitter taste and sweet, the delicious taste of the life of man, so short."

Alissa says, "I ask myself at present if it is really happiness I want, or not rather the progress toward happiness. O Lord, keep me from a happiness which I could attain too quickly! Teach me to defer, postpone until You my happiness"; and Lafcadio dreams, "One imagines *what would happen if* . . . but there always remains the little lapse through which appears the unforeseen. Nothing ever happens as one would have expected. . . . That is what makes me act. One does so little . . . *That everything be which might be,* it is thus I see creation . . . *A lover of what might be* . . ."

Gide has really invented a new form of phrase, and series of images unknown to French literature: that intense quivering of the whole being, of all the senses, which he knows how to express, that intellectual nudity, and that lucid simplicity of the mind — form in his books a magic harmony.

The rhythm which vibrates the string is well-marked, though the sound infinitely prolonged. Gide's prose pants and sings like a man under the dominion of desire. He reasons hard, to give his desire greater precision, force, acuteness. It is by desire that his books are imposed upon him, and it is from desire that his philosophy is sprung. It is for this reason that it is so new and so profound. Our seventeenth century had an analytical psychology, in which the state of repose was considered as the model, and served as a standard to judge and measure the other moments of psychic life; Romanticism had an intuitive psychology, and took sentimental revery for a model: but Gide, combining these two tendencies, and inventing, fixed the soul at the instant when it turns eagerly toward an object which it does not possess, and is not possessed by that object. This effort of man toward beings and toward the Being, halfway between nothingness and paradise, is, indeed, one of the most essential characteristics of the "human." We can never possess, but we always tend toward possession.

Gide has known how to examine this attitude, show the tension of the mind and the body, set in relief this admirable and dramatic spectacle. Thus he has given back to the spiritual life the place it ought to hold, and no one has been more of a stimulant for our generation. He has given us a doctrine for the strong: search for pleasures, search for God, search perpetual. He has been able to extend his vision to the whole universe, to contemplate all objects from this point of view. If one examines his theories it will be seen that they possess great unity and aim all at the apotheosis of desire. If he has spoken of the multiplicity of each soul, of the necessity of perpetual detachment, of infinite, absolute happiness immediately present, it is because he considers that man is destined on this earth to desire, rather than to success or renunciation.

In this there is nothing shocking or impious so long as Gide remains in dialogue with himself, or with well-armed minds and strong wills, capable of drawing stimulus from his words and not fever. For the weak, he risks being dangerous and cruel: he may lead them astray into exhausting quests, or ruin them, or disgust them. One of his qualities, and perhaps the highest, is that one cannot appreciate him properly unless he feels in himself the strength to face him and to go beyond him. But then the respect and the affection he deserves are infinite.

He has not finished his work. If he has already revealed to his contemporaries more mysteries and propounded more questions than any living modern writer, he still has his own personal problem to solve. Having installed within him a desire steadily more complete, more arrogant, he has undertaken the obligation of finding a more and more striking solution. It would be unjust to reproach him for not having yet discovered it, for his nobleness consists in his refusal to reduce, as others do, the ambitions of life to a social problem or a financial combination. But desire, like life, is only a movement, an instant. Gide will completely accomplish his undertaking only on the day (late, we hope) when he discovers the accord in which will be fused all the skillful discordances of his existence, the sacrifice or the possession which will fix forever his desires, giving them for human eternity, which we call posterity, and the other eternity, which is God, an irrefutable meaning, and an end.

Then he will be judged and we will be judged, for despite the stupid and the jealous, this generation is bound to him more than to any other.

BOOKS

A. Gide: "L'Immoraliste", "l'Enfant Prodigue", "la Porte étroite", "les Caves du Vatican", "Dostoïewski", etc.

J. Rivière: "Etudes."

Massis: "Jugements."

CHAPTER XVII

The Present State of Poetry in France
[1918–1927]

IF our poetry were to be judged from the
books in the windows of the book stores, one
would find only chaos. All kinds of verse are
written, sold, bought in France, from Baby-
lonian and Hittite poems to sequences for the
use of the year 2000. To consider Paris alone,
every class and every party has its poetry:
the Monarchist right is classic and follows the
banners of Racine, Moréas, and J. Gasquet;
the Communists and Socialists are attempting
to build up a Naturalist poetry; the University as a body seems to be Romantic (haven't
they just founded a Victor Hugo chair at the
Sorbonne?); in most of the Catholic and
moderate circles a chastened Symbolism main-
tains its influence, thanks to Jammes, Claudel,
and even Henri de Régnier (as the *Revue des
Deux Mondes* bears witness). All these poe-

159

tries coëxist, rival, penetrate, and are ignorant of one another. They agree only in crushing the works of the new generation, whom they accuse of incoherence, extravagance, absurdity. The latter in turn repudiate their elders *en bloc*, finding in this whole mass of verse nothing but tedium and wordiness. The years which have passed since 1918 have not bettered the situation. The opposition between the generations is still just as tense, and round about it the majority of the critics raise a great clamor. (See the "Chapelles littéraires" of P. Lasserre, and M. de Pierrefeu's articles in the *Journal des Débats*).

There are many causes for the prolongation of this crisis: it continues as the state of war continues, which, since 1914, has never come to an end in Europe. Suspicions, hostilities, hates, hold sway on our continent. The frontiers are insurmountable walls of brass, and numberless regulations weigh upon us. Very few of the things which maddened young men, exasperated them, drove them to revolt, have been eliminated. And on the other hand, the circles which for the past three centuries have been the principal artisans and regulators of our literature, the comfortable, well-educated bourgeois classes, have been crushed and mutilated everywhere in Europe. In France, where they have suffered a little less, their situation has become precarious.

It is not astonishing that most of the innovators and "extremists" are sprung from this class. One may say that the present crisis in poetry is a bourgeois phenomenon, just as Dada was a bourgeois School. That violence, that conscientious patience in destruction and negation are only, inverted, the old French bourgeois qualities, with their earnestness, and their love of doing well everything they do. These young men ought not, then, to be so mysterious for their elders. It was the War that made them unintelligible, by annihilating several generations, thus removing the transitions. In 1918 there were no more men of thirty, but only generals of sixty and recruits of eighteen. The adolescent found himself face to face with the old man.

And so the Schools followed one another with astonishing rapidity. Cubism flourished in 1917–1918. It possessed true poets, such as Cendrars, Reverdy, and especially Jacob. It was practiced by extraordinarily gifted writers like Cocteau, who may well be the renewer of the theater in France ("Mariés de la tour Eiffel", 1921, "Roméo et Juliette", 1924); young men like Radiguet brought it intelligence of sublime acuteness. A poetry of very intellectual construction was augured and already produced remarkable works. Suddenly it broke off short, and French poetry experienced one of the most curious and violent crises it has ever known.

Toward 1917 was born at Zurich a monster named "Dada", whose parents were a Roumanian (Tzara), a German Alsatian (Arp), and a German (Huelsenbeck). This group launched a doctrine which soon had a brilliant and scandalous success. For its diffusion, it found in France a nucleus of young men as gifted in intelligence as in sensibility, and it was quickly evident that it corresponded to a very profound instinct in the new generation. This School was at first only the continuation of literary Cubism, an attempt to create a poetic world in opposition to the material world, and freed of its tutelage, but it ended by revolting against Cubism as against everything on earth.

Dada did not confine itself to the denial of the value and the existence of things; its denial included everything: society, public, vocabulary, intelligence, literature. In one sense it was the extreme point of Romanticism, for it proclaimed the bankruptcy of reason and society; it declared that if a man was a poet, everything that he said spontaneously was poetry. That was to affirm the absolute supremacy of inspiration. The object of Dada was not so much to be understood as to impress. Judging that all our words, our entire civilization, were only deception and misunderstanding, it pretended to aim solely at an "acceptable misunderstanding." Certain of these writers produced really beautiful works: the lyric verses of Tzara, the "Champs magnétiques" (1920) of Breton and Soupault will doubtless last. Paul Eluard has written little poems that are unforgettable. But the general public knew of Dada hardly more than its clamors: public meetings, manifestoes, the Barrès trial, etc. For them Dada was a group of desperadoes in search of notoriety, drama, despair, and mortal glory.

On the world of letters Dada made a deep impression. The phenomenon appeared suddenly. But it was not unintelligible. Since Rimbaud's retirement and the death of Lautréamont it might have been foreseen that a spasm of this kind would be experienced in France. Exalted ambitions, demands without limit, sensibility refined to the point of torture, an abstract, profound, and insurgent idealism, passionate, indistinct mysticism — all these things we cultivated and found nothing to satisfy, were bound to lead to a great declaration of bankruptcy on the day when some part or other of our civilization gave way. Our country was working to create marvels of elegance and sensibility such as no race had known since the Greeks, and at the same time establishing a social order which was the most precise, the most unyielding, the most strict, centralized and unified that had ever existed. (Since Napoleon, the stricter and stricter organizing and disciplining of France has continued without interruption.) This was to doom to death whatever was best in us. The sedition that was Dada led to destruction some of the noblest minds of that time — it aided them and drove them to disappear. It is stained with a blood that makes it shine. If I have spoken of this movement, it is because of them.

Dada made so much noise that it was lost in the clamor. The imprecation "I am going to die" is terrible and beautiful when it is followed by death; if it is a means to live it becomes boring, as dramatics. Dada worked its own destruction by lasting. But it destroyed a great deal around it. It gave a precise form to our disgusts. By pushing Romanticism to its limit, Dada brought it to a close, and made it seem tiresome, even at its most brilliant, as in Mme. de Noailles. It has left us only two resources: either the noble triumph of spirituality, such as in the "Défense de Tartufe", by Max Jacob, and in "Charmes", by Valéry, or a pleasure of the body, not simply devoted to voluptuousness,

as would have been possible in 1913, but
active, taut, enjoying its fatigue as much as its
extension, as is to be seen in the sport poetry
born recently from a sort of reaction against
the odor of death which emanated from Dada.
Henry de Montherlant has brought into this
genre magnificent poetical talents not always
worthily served by his intelligence. If these
two forms of poetry are flourishing and have
profited by the crisis, one may say that its influence has been felt everywhere. (attempt to
create an epigrammatic poetry, the *haïkaï*,
the quatrain mode, in which the "Soirées de
Pétrograd", real masterpiece by Chalupt, is
the greatest success).

In 1925–1926 was even seen to develop an
offshoot of Dada, Surréalisme, formed from
about the same elements, but after those
elements had experienced the influence of
Freud and Russian communism. Surréalisme
is at the moment the most daring, the most
violent literary School in France. Going beyond the social and worldly appearances in
the midst of which we live, it pretends to express a profounder reality, a *surréalité* whose

dwelling place and source is to be found in the most mysterious part, deepest in the sub-conscious of our being. For the *Surréaliste* the task has ceased to be the discovery of ideas or the writing of poetry; he aims solely to let speak through him that mysterious voice, thrusting aside all logic, all convention, all morality even, which might restrict its absolute liberty and spontaneity.

One after the other, Cubism and Dada, through their great qualities as through their odious, have served to preserve the impulse given to French poetry by Rimbaud in its original direction and force: a *chasse spirituelle*, in search of the purest world, the freest, and the most within. Doubtless these schools have as a rule forced the writers to solitude and individualism, but that is not too great a misfortune from the artistic point of view. Everything cannot or ought not be intelligible to everybody. It is well that there be clearly marked boundaries. A poetry that would rise high must not address too numerous a public. Such a discipline, increasing the dignity of the poet and accentuating his personality, is the discipline of a great epoch. If one considers the number of our poets, their quality, and the poetic genres they cultivate, one is bound to conclude that France has rarely known a development of pure poetry (that is, distinguished from eloquence, music, theater) comparable to that which we now admire. Not since the seventeenth century, doubtless, have we created a poetry so personal, strong, virile, and so much our own.

BOOKS

Tzara: "Cinéma. . ."

A. Breton and Ph. Soupault: "Les Champs magnétiques."

Jacob: "La Défense de Tartufe."

Cendrars: "Le Panama."

H. de Montherlant: "Le Songe."

CHAPTER XVIII

The Present State of French Prose
[1918–1927]

FRENCH prose, docile always to social influences, did not fail to be convulsed by the War. Besides, by 1914 it had reached the limit beyond which there can be no pleasant sensations. The War, with its train of brutalities and violence, drove it to the search for harsh impressions. In vain a certain number sought, rather artificially, to revive the taste for pleasure and emotion, as did Mauriac with ingenious talent; in vain others like Benoit attempted to resurrect the novel of adventure: they hardly carried the public. Their success, sometimes bright, nevertheless pales in comparison with the triumph of Barbusse with "le Feu." This book possessed emphasis rather than literary qualities, and it came at its time. It was followed by a whole literature, interesting but painful, and bearing the impress of the moral and social suffering which we have known from 1914 to this day (the books of G. Duhamel, Dorgelès, Pierre Hamp).

By the side of this group a mass of good writers entered the same field, as bear witness the fine books of J. R. Bloch, "l'Esprit Impur" of Gilbert de Voisins, the "Thibault" of Martin du Gard, "la Brière" of Chateaubriant. A sort of mode drove toward the macabre. A fantastic Naturalism was invented, out of which Mac Orlan and Salmon drew a number of original effects. They founded almost a School, while on a less lofty tone, Henry Béraud described the martyrdom of the Fat Man and the sad fate of Lazare. All these writers, of very unequal qualities, made an impression on the public and got themselves read, but no one of them was able to impose himself as leader upon the new generation. Despite the formation of the group "Clarté" and undeniable popular sympathies for these authors, this return of Naturalism or Realism into our civilization seems to be little more than a manifestation, hardly original, of a tendency which is constant in our literature.

It was not sufficient to galvanize our prose, hampered by the economic difficulties in which we are struggling (rise of the price of books, impoverishment of the middle classes), hampered also by the attitude of poetry and by the transformation of the French language. This last, in fact, was passing through a formidable crisis. The War had changed the meaning of words (especially those denoting ideas and sentiments) and also the domain of French. Until then, in fact, French, the recognized diplomatic language, had possessed in Europe a clientèle at the same time elegant (the higher classes in Russia, Germany, Poland, Austria), bourgeois (in the same countries), and commercial (especially in the Orient). It felt the influence of those who spoke it, and was turned, then, toward the East. The long struggle closed those regions to us, where political hatreds and the rate of exchange no longer allowed our books to circulate; on the other hand it gave us the immense Anglo-Saxon public. This race, in process of becoming ruler of the sea, banker of the world, and thus the arbiter of peace, learned to love French, to speak it, and to court our modes. At the moment when the Anglo-Saxons won the hegemony and imposed English everywhere as the commercial and political language, they adopted French as a literary dialect. The whole West opened to our professors and litterateurs. At the same time Americanism held sway with us. This new orientation of our tastes affected our vocabulary, which was enriched with strange words, and which lost in clarity. As poetry at the same time was tending by its daring methods to tear down the traditional logic on which was based the grammar of our country, our prose writers found themselves in cruel embarrassment. Now the before-the-War prose sounded hollow, gave a painful impression of lacking density, of being antiquated, but it is not easy to invent an instrument and adapt it suddenly to new uses.

A certain number felt this change of demands and tendencies at the same time as the public, and hastened to explore the domains that were opening. Jean Giraudoux and Paul Morand have attempted, thanks to marvelous sensibility, very cleverly exploited, to discover a whole fabric of images suitable to our modern life and our position as "cosmopolitan aristocrats." Giraudoux, turning alternately toward America, which he knows well, and Germany, which he has understood, wrote those books of charming brilliances, "Suzanne et le Pacifique", "Siegfried et le Limousin." His ease of bearing, and his generous and varied sensibility, have contributed to give him a rôle of initiator. Morand, his friend and colleague, has succeeded even better. He has perhaps less talent, but his dexterity and intelligence make it up: out of our poor bleeding Europe he has drawn a complete picturesque, modern and amusing. He has even divined and attempted what should be the work of to-morrow: to find beyond this picturesque the common ideas and essential differences which constitute the value of our rival and related civilizations. He has thrown into the ring more comparisons, anecdotes, wit, and pictures than any other of the new generation.

One can already be sure that he will remain as one of the most typical story-tellers of our time, for if he has a weakness, it lies in the very excess of his cleverness, which makes him perceive too clearly the character of the present moment, and gives a dangerous touch of actuality to all his works.

In the company of these writers, there is a whole group, very distinguished, who strive toward an analogous goal, the rejuvenation of French prose, but would reach it by a different route. Basing themselves especially on modern poetry, they aim to carry over its methods and tendencies into the prose. Their best arm is the voluntary, simplifying, and creative intelligence. This light shines with incomparable brilliance in the "Thomas l'Imposteur" of Jean Cocteau, whose forceful gravity I much admire. But there are three young writers who have succeeded better than all the rest in this difficult undertaking. A. Aragon in his "Anicet" (and his "Paysan de Paris") has treated the external world as a theme, a possibility susceptible of being conceived and described in many different ways.

He has thus written a modern fairy tale which is the triumph of the imagination. Marcel Jouhandeau, in "Les Pincengrain", has described the dismal, secretly exalted existence of the small towns. Into the painting and the analysis he has been able to put so profound a sense of spiritual life, allied with such hot voluptuousness and such a direct comprehension of character, that the book presents a unique combination of pious clairvoyance and sensual aberration. Raymond Radiguet, unhappy child of genius, has created a sublime and voluntary psychology in the "Diable au corps" and the "Bal du Comte d'Orgel." Everything in these books is fiction, choice, and aims at the creation of a world, at the reproduction of nothing. The introduction, even into the description of characters, of the fancies of the author, is a feat which promises marvels.

Death interrupted Radiguet at the moment when he was about to win an audience. Others will continue and profit by these efforts. They will be helped by those publishers who are anxious to dissipate the misunderstanding of the present hour and reveal to the masses the best and boldest of our contemporary writers. If they succeed, they will bring French prose back to its true place, the French nation, without spoiling its world influence, or that sincere inspiration which constitutes its dignity. This is not an easy task. Prevailing over the indecision of the public, the disorder of minds, our prose writers must impose a dictatorship, for at this moment there is need of a fresh vocabulary, a newly defined universe, and an original psychology. It is not enough to begin anew, but just as in 1650–1660 Frenchmen were brought together only through a violent exercise of reason and will, so in our day only a bold imagination, resolute, heroic, shall we say, can rally minds no longer persuaded or satisfied by their senses, and wearied by their reason.

If they do not fail these generations will be very great. For the task ahead is appalling. Their mad desires, unlimited needs, the ruins which surround them, everything within and without seems to conspire to smother them.

Will we succeed in satisfying ourselves, and in creating for the world that art which it expects from us? In spite of death, misunderstanding, ennui, ridicule, I have wagered that we will.

I am done. There are many more names to pronounce and writers to praise, for France is rich in talents, and eighteen chapters will scarce suffice to present a complete image of everything that is happening in modern French literature. I will leave that to others. My object was to give a clear and schematic picture of what I call "to-day." I wanted to aid in the perception of the unique and passing odor of the days which we are living. I have not allowed myself to talk about everything which I love and esteem, my function seeming not so much the disclosure of authors as the discovery of tendencies; but I am sorry that I cannot say the good I think of a Daniel Halévy, a Georges Sorel, a Lafont, a Duhamel, a Vildrac, and many others. Above all I have desired to call attention to a few facts, a small number of writers that I considered particularly ours. Nothing is sadder, more stupid, than for men to let themselves live and disappear without knowing. At least let not this parable be applied to us:

"But whereunto shall I liken this generation? It is like unto children sitting in the markets, and calling unto their fellows, and saying, We have piped unto you, and ye have not danced; we have mourned unto you, and ye have not lamented."

BOOKS

J. Giraudoux: "Suzanne et le Pacifique."
P. Morand: "Ouvert la nuit."
Aragon: "Anicet."
R. Radiguet: "Le Bal du Comte d'Orgel."
J. Cocteau: "Thomas l'Imposteur."
M. Jouhandeau: "Les Pincengrain."

END